The Great Retreat, 1914

The Great Retreat, 1914

Two Accounts of the Battle & Retreat From
Mons by the B.E.F., During the First World War

The Retreat from Mons

George Stuart Gordon

The Fighting Retreat to Paris

Roger Ingpen

LEONAUR

The Great Retreat, 1914
Two Accounts of the Battle & Retreat From Mons by the B.E.F.,
During the First World War
The Retreat from Mons
by George Stuart Gordon
The Fighting Retreat to Paris
by Roger Ingpen

FIRST EDITION

First published under the titles
The Retreat from Mons
and
The Fighting Retreat to Paris

Leonaur is an imprint
of Oakpast Ltd

ISBN: 978-1-78282-327-8 hardcover)
ISBN: 978-1-78282-328-5 (softcover)

http://www.leonaur.com

Publisher's Notes
The views expressed in this book are not necessarily
those of the publisher.

Contents

The Retreat from Mons

Contents

Preface

I am told that it has been thought advisable to publish short accounts in pamphlet form of prominent and important operations which have been carried on during the course of the war which is still raging.

Such war stories may undoubtedly be beneficial, and in the belief that such "propaganda" is productive of more good than harm I have consented to indite this very brief preface to *The Retreat from Mons*.

Any hesitation I may have felt arises from my profound conviction that no history of a war or any part of a war can be worth anything until some period after peace has been made and the full facts are known and understood.

This work however, is not so much a "history" as an interesting summary or a chronology of leading events, and the writer carefully avoids according praise or blame in connection with any event or group of events which can ever become the subject of controversy.

In a preface to so brief and so unpretentious a military work as this, it is impossible to put before the reader more than a glimpse of the situation in regard to which plans had to be conceived and put into execution as suddenly and speedily as the demand for them was unexpected.

That it is the "unexpected" which generally happens in war, and that it is the "unexpected" for which we must be ever ready, has of late years been deeply instilled in the mind of the British officer. A cardinal axiom in his military creed is that he must never be taken by surprise.

When, therefore, the Germans, on the same principle as they subsequently used poison-gas, sank hospital ships, and disregarded every known rule of civilized war, suddenly and quite unexpectedly overran a neutral country in such a drastic manner as to nullify all preconceived plans and possibilities, and the British Army found itself on the outer flank of the threatened line exposed to the full weight of the German menace, it was this previous careful training which formed the sure foundation upon which to plan and conduct the inevitable retreat and carry it to a successful conclusion.

When men are told to retire without fighting, when they see no reason for it, when they remain full of ardour and longing to get at the enemy, and are not allowed to, demoralization is very apt to be the result. Why was such a feature of the Retreat conspicuous by its complete non-existence? Because of another result of British military training, namely, the absolute confidence of the men in their leaders and officers and the wonderful mutual understanding which existed between them.

The magnificent spirit which animated the British Expeditionary Force was seen at every phase of these operations; in the skilful handling and moral superiority of the cavalry which covered the Retreat; in the able conduct by the respective leaders of the several battles and encounters which local circumstances rendered necessary; and lastly, in the extraordinary marching powers and capability of endurance which animated all ranks.

Controversies loud and bitter will certainly rage in regard to all the dispositions and plans under which this war has been conducted; as to the operations of the first three weeks, perhaps, more than as to those of any other period.

But I venture to hope and believe that no sane person can dispute in the smallest particular the claims which I make in this very short preface on behalf of the forces which it is the great pride and glory of my life to have commanded.

French
F.M.

Whitehall
April 23, 1917.

Introductory

The first quality of British military operations in the present war—and so it will strike the future historian—is their astonishing variety and range. Beginning on the ancient battlefields of France and Flanders, they have spread, in a series of expanding and apparently inevitable waves, over a good part of three continents, so that, wherever the enemy was to be found,—whether in Europe, or Asia, or Africa, or in the islands of the high seas,—there also, sooner or later, were the British arms. There was a time when one or two campaigns were thought amply sufficient for the military energies of the most warlike nation. We have never pretended to be warlike, meeting our emergencies always, with a certain reluctance, as they arose; but in the present war we have seldom had fewer than six considerable campaigns on our hands at one time, and these in areas separated often by thousands of miles from one another and from us.

It is one of the obligations of a great empire at war that it should be so; it is one of the privileges of a great maritime empire that it should be possible. It is undoubtedly the grand characteristic of the operations of the British Army in this war, and gives the only true perspective of our military effort in the field. To our share in the Allied front must always be added the fighting frontiers of the Empire.

The British Army, now grown out of all recognition, was small, and known to be small, when the war began. It was a voluntary army, numbering approximately 700,000 men, of whom about 450,000 (including reservists) were trained soldiers, liable for service abroad, and the remainder, a half-trained Territorial Force, enrolled for service at home. Besides being small, it was, from the nature of its duties, widely scattered. Over 100,000 of our best troops were serving at the time in India or on foreign stations. For all purposes, therefore, when war broke out, we had in this country a mobilisable army of something under 600,000 trained and half-trained men, 250,000 of whom were liable only for service at home. The striking or Expeditionary Force of this army was a fully equipped and highly professional body of six infantry divisions and one division of cavalry, and with this force we entered the war. Intended primarily, as its name implied, for protective or punitive operations within the Empire, it was on a scale proportionate to its purpose and to the size of our army.

Our army, judged by a European standard, being small, our Expeditionary Force, judged by that standard, was diminutive; and the chief problem which confronted the government, when it was decided to send this force to France, was how to support and supplement it. The story of how this problem was faced and overcome, of how "Home Service" men became "Foreign Service" in a day, and our little army of 700,000, by a gigantic effort of British determination and Imperial goodwill, was expanded into an army of millions all this is a separate narrative, to be related elsewhere; but we cannot afford to overlook it as we follow the fortunes of the Expeditionary Force in France and Flanders. It is the military background of all their triumphs and vicissitudes, and had an effect upon the tone of the war almost from the first. Even to our Expeditionary Force itself, with all its cheerful self-confidence and efficiency, it meant something to know that the country was in earnest; that as early as August 23, while they were still fighting among the coal-pits of Mons, the first 100,000 volunteers had been enrolled, and were already deep in the mysteries of forming fours.

The Retreat from Mons

When a country goes to war the first test of its military efficiency is the mobilisation of its army. This is a stage in the history of wars which the public is apt to overlook, because the arrangements are necessarily secret and complex, and are carried out in that first hush which precedes *communiqués* and great conflicts in the field. It is nevertheless true that every war starts in the Department of the Quartermaster General, and that by the nature of this start the issue of a war may be decided. We started well. From August 5, when mobilisation began,—in spite of bank holidays and Territorials *en route* for summer camps,—the whole scheme of concentration and despatch was carried out almost exactly to schedule, and without a hitch. It is calculated that, during the busiest period, the railway companies, now under government control and brilliantly directed by an executive committee of general managers, were able to run as many as eighteen hundred special trains in five days, an average of three hundred and sixty trains a day, and all up to time.

The concentration of the Home Forces and of the Expeditionary Force proceeded concurrently. On August 9 the first elements of the force embarked, and nine days later the greater part of it had been landed in France, and was moving by way of Amiens to its unknown fortunes. The smoothness, rapidity, above all the secrecy with which the transportation was carried out, made a great impression at the time, and will always be admired. The question of how it was done excited, characteristically enough, less interest. We are a people accustomed to happy improvisations, and it was generally assumed that this national talent had once more come to our rescue; the truth being that in these matters improvisation can seldom be happy, and that for instant and complete success the only method is long and careful preparation in time of peace. For several years the military, naval, and

GERMANS ADVANCING AT MONS

civilian authorities concerned had been engaged upon such a scheme of preparation, and had, indeed, concluded their labours not many months before war broke out.

When the day came all railway and naval transport officers were at their posts, and the Railway Executive Committee, in its offices in Parliament Street, was calmly carrying out a time-table with every detail of which it had long been familiar. Such perfect preparedness is rare in our history, and worthy of note. Amidst the vast unreadiness of the nation for war the despatch of the Expeditionary Force, and the magnificent readiness of the fleet which made it possible, stand out in grand relief, not to be lost sight of or forgotten.

The Expeditionary Force was commanded by Field Marshal Sir John French, and consisted, up to August 23, of four complete divisions of infantry (the First, Second, Third, and Fifth) and five brigades of cavalry; that is to say, about 80,000 men. On August 24 it was joined by the Nineteenth Infantry Brigade, which added 4000 more; and on August 25 by the Fourth Division, which added another 17,000. Our total strength, therefore, during the fighting at Mons and in the Retreat, varied from 80,000 to a little over 100,000 men. It was a small force, but of a quality rarely seen. No finer fighting unit ever entered the field. In physique and equipment, in professional training and experience of war, in that quality of skilful and cheerful tenacity against odds which distinguishes the veteran, it was probably unrivalled by any body of troops of its time. The French, who gave our men a warm welcome, dwell always on their youth and good spirits, their wonderful cleanness and healthiness, the excellence of their equipment, and their universal courtesy.

A French infantryman who fought in the Retreat and on the Marne writes:

> À Argenteuil-Triage, nous croisons un train de fantassins anglais; figures rasées, ouvertes, enfantines, riant de toutes leurs dents. Ils sont reluisants de propreté. Nous nous acclamons réciproquement. (Sept. 2/14: Carnet de Route; Roujons.)

At Bucy-le-long the French relieve the English. It is a matter of outposts.

> De deux cents mètres en deux cents mètres, un groupe de six Anglais est couché à plat ventre dans les betteraves, en bordure d'un chemin. Ils se dressent et nous allons prendre leurs places en admirant ces beaux soldats, bien équipés, silencieux, et qui ont des couvertures. (Ibid., Oct. 6/14.)

British Infantry marching

Such opinions were worth much. For though it is a great thing to be welcomed, as our men were welcomed, by a whole people, to have the hearty professional approval of its soldiers is a greater thing still.

The Expeditionary Force, thus landed in France, was organised in two army corps—the First, consisting of the First and Second Divisions, under Lieutenant-General Sir Douglas Haig; the second, consisting of the Third and Fifth Divisions, under Lieutenant-General Sir James Grierson, who was succeeded, on his sudden and much lamented death, by General Sir Horace Smith-Dorrien. General Allenby commanded the cavalry division, consisting of the First, Second, Third, and Fourth Cavalry Brigades, and the Fifth Cavalry Brigade was commanded independently by Brigadier-General Sir Philip Chetwode. By the evening of Friday, August 21, the concentration was practically complete, and during Saturday the 22d the Force moved up to its position on the left or western extremity of the French line. (Plan 1.)

The general situation in this region, as it was known at the moment to the leaders of the Allies, may be briefly stated. It was at last plain, after much uncertainty, that the first great shock and collision of forces was destined to take place in this northern area. It was plain, also, that Belgium, for some time to come, was out of the scheme. Liège had fallen, and with it how many hopes and predictions of the engineer! Brussels was occupied; and the Belgian field army was retiring to shelter under the ramparts of Antwerp. Except for Namur, there was nothing in Belgium north of the Allied line to stop the German advance. Von Kluck and Von Buelow, with the First and Second German Armies, were marching without opposition towards the French frontier—Von Kluck towards the southwest and Von Buelow towards the crossings of the Sambre. By the evening of the 20th, Von Buelow's guns were bombarding Namur. So much was known to the leaders of the Allies: of the strength of the advancing armies they knew little.

To oppose these two armies—for of the seven German armies already in position we shall consider only these two—the Allies were disposed as follows: Directly in the route of Von Buelow's army, should he pass Namur, lay the Fifth French Army, under General Lanrezac, with its left resting on the River Sambre at Charleroi, and its right in the fork of the Meuse and the Sambre. This army, it should be noted, made a junction in the river fork with another French Army, the Fourth, under General Ruffey, which lay off to the south along the Middle Meuse, watching the Ardennes. On the left of the Fifth

French Army, along a line presently to be defined, lay the British Expeditionary Force, facing, as it seemed, with equal directness, the line of advance of the army of Von Kluck.

Subsidiary to the Fifth French Army and the British Force were two formations, available for support: a cavalry corps of three divisions under General Sordet, stationed to the south of Maubeuge, and, out to the west, with its base at Arras, a corps of two reserve divisions under General D'Amade. Both these formations will be heard of during the subsequent operations, and it is important to remark that General D'Amade's two divisions were at this time, and throughout the first days of the fighting, the only considerable body of Allied troops in the eighty miles of territory between the British and the sea.

The line occupied by the British ran due east from the neighbourhood of Condé along the straight of the Condé-Mons Canal, round the loop which the canal makes north of Mons, and then, with a break, patrolled by cavalry, turned back at almost a right angle towards the southeast of the direction of the Mons-Beaumont road. The whole of the canal line, including the loop round Mons,—a front of nearly twenty miles,—was held by the Second Army Corps, and the First Army Corps lay off to its right, holding the south-eastern line to a point about nine miles from Mons. There being no infantry reserves available in this small force, General Allenby's cavalry division was employed to act on the flank or in support of any threatened part of the line. The forward reconnaissance was entrusted to the Fifth Cavalry Brigade, assisted by some squadrons from General Allenby's division, and some of its detachments penetrated as far north as Soignies, nine miles on the way to Brussels. In the occasional encounters which took place with the enemy's *Uhlans*, to the north and east, our cavalry had always the best of it; then, as always in this war, when the opportunity has occurred, mounted or dismounted, they have proved themselves the better arm. Their reconnaissance was more than supplemented by four squadrons of the Royal Flying Corps under the direction of Major-General Sir David Henderson.

Throughout the Saturday our men entrenched themselves, the North-Countrymen among them finding in the chimney-stacks and slag-heaps of this mining district much to remind them of home. The line they held was clearly not an easy line to defend. No salient ever is, and a glance at the map will show that this was no common salient. To the sharp apex of Mons was added, as an aggravation, the loop of the canal. It was nevertheless the best line available, and, once adopted, had been occupied with that double view both to defence and to attack which a good commander has always before him. The first object, when an enemy of unknown strength attacks, is to hold him and gain time; the line of the canal supplies just the obstacle required; it was therefore held, in spite of the salient, and arrangements made for a withdrawal of the Second Corps should the salient become untenable.

If, on the other hand, the enemy should be beaten back, the Second Corps, pivoting northeast on Mons, could cross the canal and move forward in line with the First Corps, already in position for such an advance. If, finally,—for a commander, like a good parent, must provide for everything,—a general retirement should become necessary, the British commander-in-chief had decided to rest his right flank on Maubeuge, twelve miles south of Mons: and here was his First Corps ready for it, clustered about the roads that lead towards Maubeuge, and able, from this advantage, to cover the retirement of the Second Corps, which had fewer facilities in this way, and would have farther to travel. Tactically the arrangements were as good as could be made.

When we come to the strength and direction of the enemy's attack, we are on more doubtful ground. His strength on the British front was estimated at the time, according to all the available information, both French and English, to be at most two army corps, with perhaps one cavalry division, which would have made an equal battle; and it was not unnaturally supposed that he would attack in the general direction of his advance; that is, from the northeast. From an attack in this strength and from this direction we had nothing to fear. As it turned out, however, both the estimate of strength and the supposition of direction were inaccurate. The enemy, making full use of the wooded country in these parts, which gave excellent concealment, and strong enough to throw his forces wide, was, as we shall see, engaged on something much more ambitious; a movement which, had it succeeded (as against any other troops it might well have succeeded), would have brought disaster on the whole Allied army.

At what hour precisely the Germans began their attack on the Mons position is uncertain. Some say at dawn, others just after noon. What is certain is that between 12 and 1 p.m. on Sunday the 23rd, some of the men of the Royal West Kents, in support on the outskirts of Mons, were having a sing-song and watching the people home from church, and, feeling quite at their ease, had sent their shirts and socks out to wash, for all the world as if on manoeuvres. It is an interesting little scene, and one which would have seemed incomprehensible to the Germans, who by this time pictured our little army cowering in its positions. The abruptness with which the scene changed is no less characteristic.

When it was reported that the enemy had turned up "at last" and that "A" company was hard-pressed at the canal, there was no more thought of sing-songs nor even of the dinner "which the orderlies had just gone to fetch"; socks and shirts appeared as if by miracle; and when the "fall-in" went, every man was there, equipped and ready for anything. It is an ordinary incident, and for that reason important; in any institution, whether it be an army or a household, it is the ordinary incidents that count. It is typical of the spirit of an army which has puzzled many even of its admirers by its strange combination of qualities: boyish ease and hilarity coupled with manly fortitude and discipline, and a most perfect and unassailable confidence in its weapons, its leaders, and itself.

The attack had most certainly begun; and it began, as was expected, at the weakest and most critical point of the line, the canal loop, which was held by the Third Division. This division had the heaviest share of the fighting throughout the day, maintaining, longer than seemed humanly possible, a hopeless position against hopeless odds, the Second Royal Irish and Fourth Middlesex of the Eighth Brigade, and the Fourth Royal Fusiliers of the Ninth Brigade, particularly distinguishing themselves. The bridges over the canal, which our men held, after some preliminary shelling, were attacked by infantry debouching from the low woods which at this point came down to within three hundred or four hundred yards of the canal. These woods were of great assistance to the enemy, both here and at other points of the canal, in providing cover for their infantry and machine-guns. The odds were very heavy. One company of the Royal Fusiliers, holding the Nimy Bridge, was attacked at one time by as many as four battalions.

The enemy at first came on in masses, and suffered severely in consequence. It was their first experience of the British "fifteen rounds a minute," and it told. They went down in bundles—our men delighting in a form of musketry never contemplated in the Regulations. To men accustomed to hitting bobbing heads at eight hundred yards there was something monstrous and incredible in the German advance. They could scarcely believe their eyes; such targets had never appeared to them even in their dreams.

Nor were our machine-guns idle. In this, as in many other actions that day and in the days that followed, our machine-guns were handled with a skill and devotion which no one appreciated more than the enemy. Two of the first Victoria Crosses of the war were won by machine-gunners in this action of the bridges: Lieutenant Dease, of the Royal Fusiliers, who, though five times wounded,—and, as it turned out, mortally wounded,—continued to work his gun on the Nimy Bridge until the order came for retirement, and he was carried off; and Private Godley, of the Royal Scots Fusiliers, who, lower down the loop, at the Ghlin Bridge, in the face of repeated assaults, kept his gun in action throughout.

The attack had now spread along the whole line of the canal; but except at the loop the enemy could make no impression. There, however, numbers told at last, and about the middle of the afternoon the Third Division was ordered to retire from the salient, and the Fifth Division on its left directed to conform. Bridges were blown up—the Royal Engineers vying with the other services in the race for glory: and by the night of the 23rd, after various vicissitudes, the Second Army Corps had fallen back as far as the line Montreuil-Wasmes-Paturages-Frameries. That the retirement, though successful, was expensive, is not to be wondered at, when it is remembered that throughout this action, as we now know, the Second Army Corps was outnumbered by three to one. All ranks, however, were in excellent spirits. Allowing for handicaps, they felt that they had proved themselves the better men.

It was a feeling which was to be severely tried in the next few days. At 5 p.m. on Sunday the 23rd, as the Second Corps was withdrawing from the canal, the British commander-in-chief received a most unexpected telegram from General Joffre, the *generalissimo* of the Allied armies, to the effect that at least three German army corps were moving against the British front, and that a fourth corps was endeavouring to outflank him from the west. He was also informed that the Germans had on the previous day captured the crossings of the Sambre between Charleroi and Namur, and that the French on his right were retiring. In other words, Namur, the defensive pivot of the Anglo-French line, on the resistance of which—if only for a few days—the Allied strategy had depended, had fallen almost at a blow. By Saturday the Germans had left Namur behind, and in numbers far exceeding French predictions had seized the crossings of the Sambre and Middle Meuse and were hammering at the junction of the Fifth and Fourth French Armies in the river-fork.

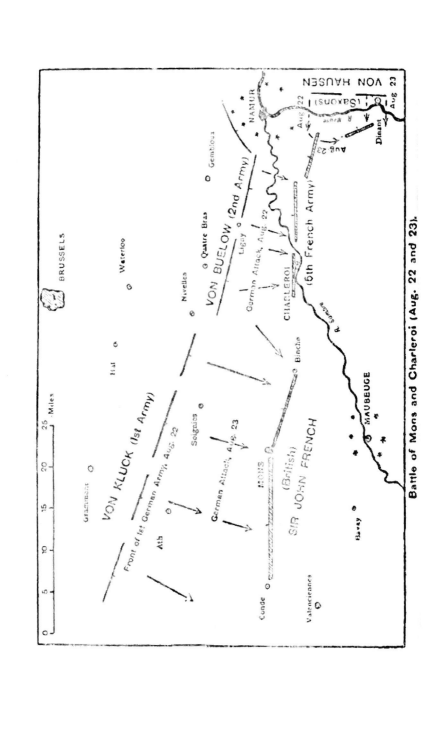

Battle of Mons and Charleroi (Aug. 22 and 23).

The junction was pierced, and the French, unexpectedly and overwhelmingly assaulted both in front and flank, could do nothing but retire. By 5 p.m. on the Sunday, when the message was received at British Headquarters, the French had been retiring for anywhere from ten to twelve hours. The British Army was for the moment isolated. Standing forward a day's march from the French on its right, faced and engaged by three German corps in front, and already threatened by a fourth corps on its left, it seemed a force marked out for destruction.

In the British Higher Command, however, there was no flurry. There is a thing called British phlegm.

The facts of the case, though unwelcome, were laconically accepted. Over General Headquarters brooded a clubroom calm. Airmen were sent up to confirm the French report, in the usual manner, and arrangements were quietly and methodically made for a retirement towards the prearranged Maubeuge-Valenciennes line. The hard-pressed Second Corps, which had farther to march, was the first to move. Early on the 24th it was marching south towards Dour and Quarouble, covered by the First Corps, which had been much less taxed, and was favourably placed to threaten the German left. This covering demonstration was well carried out by the Second Division, supported by the massed artillery of the corps. The retirement of the Second Corps, however, even with this assistance, was not made without much difficulty. By the night of the 23rd the enemy were already crossing the canal, and pouring down on the villages to the south.

Several rear-guard actions were fought here on the morning of the 24th, in which infantry and artillery equally distinguished themselves at Wasmes with notable success and much loss to the enemy; but, as every hour passed, the intention of the enemy to outflank from the northwest became more evident. Desperate fighting took place, the First Norfolks, First Cheshires, and One Hundred and Nineteenth Battery, R.F.A., detached as a flank guard under Colonel Ballard, of the Norfolks, holding the ridge from Audregnies to Flouges for several hours in the teeth of overwhelming opposition. To this little band, which cheerfully sacrificed itself, belongs the principal credit for holding up the turning movement of the enemy during the retirement of the 24th. They made a splendid stand, and six hundred of the Cheshires never got away.

Our cavalry, fortunately, were able to help also, and at once; for by an act of great foresight, long before the news arrived of a turning movement, Sir John French had transferred his cavalry division from the right flank to the left. They were in position there by the Sunday morning, and in the subsequent retirement did everything that men and horses could do to relieve the pressure. The dramatic action of General de Lisle's cavalry brigade at Audregnies, where the Fifth Division was hard-pressed, is one of the best-known incidents of this day's fighting, not only because it succeeded, though at a heavy cost, in delaying the enemy, but because it gave occasion to one of the most heroic performances of the Retreat.

When the action was drawing to a close, and men, horses, and batteries were being withdrawn, Captain Francis Grenfell, of the Ninth Lancers, observed that the One Hundred and Nineteenth Battery, R.F.A., was in difficulties. All the horses of the battery had been killed, most of its personnel had been killed or wounded, and it looked as if the guns would have to be left. Captain Grenfell, though himself wounded, determined to help, and rode out to look for a way of retreat for the guns. Having found it, to show how little a cavalryman need care for death, he rode his horse back, under a tempest of fire, at a walk, and called for volunteers from the lancers, reminding them that "the Ninth had never failed the gunners." After such an example the response could be nothing but brisk. He returned with his volunteers ("eleven officers and some forty men"), and under a fierce and incessant fire the guns were manhandled into safety. For this fine action Captain Grenfell and the battery commander—Major Alexander—were each awarded the Victoria Cross. It is one of many illustrations furnished by the Retreat of the *camaraderie* of the various arms.

After a short halt and partial entrenchment on the line Dour-Quarouble, to enable the First Corps to break off its demonstrations, the retreat of the Second Corps was resumed; and by the evening of the 24th the whole army had reached the prearranged line Jenlain-Bavai-Maubeuge—the Second Corps to the west of Bavai, and the First Corps to the right. The right was protected by the fortress of Maubeuge, the left by the cavalry, operating outwards, and by the Nineteenth Infantry Brigade, which had been brought up in the nick of time from the lines of communication, and had acted throughout the day in support of the exposed flank of the Second Corps.

It had been intended by the British commander-in-chief to make a stand on the Maubeuge line, and if the first calculations of the enemy's strength and intentions had proved correct, it is possible that a great battle might have been fought here, and continued by the French armies along the whole fortress line of northern France. Even as it was, the temptation to linger at Maubeuge must have been strong; it offered such an inviting buttress to our right flank, and filled so comfortably that dangerous gap between our line and the French. The temptation, to which a weaker commander might have succumbed, was resisted. The despatch says:

> The French were still retiring, and I had no support except such as was afforded by the fortress of Maubeuge; and the determined attempts of the enemy to get round my left flank assured me that it was his intention to hem me against that place and surround me. I felt that not a moment must be lost in retiring to another position.

Early on the 25th, accordingly, the whole British Army set out on the next stage of its retreat. Its function in the general Allied strategy was now becoming clear. It was not merely fighting its own battles. Situated as it was on the left flank of the retiring French Armies, it had become in effect the left flank-guard of the Allied line, committed to its retirement, and to the protection of that retirement, to the end. The turning movement from the west, at first local and partial, had suddenly acquired a strategic significance. It threatened not merely the British Army, but the whole Allied strategy of the Retreat. Could the British resist it? Could they, at the least, delay it? These were the questions which the French leaders asked themselves, with some anxiety, as they retired with their armies from day to day, and waited for the counter-turn which was to come. For, as we now know, behind the retiring and still intact French Armies, to the south and east of Paris, movements were shaping, forces were forming, which were to change the face of things in this western corner. Could the British hold out till these movements were ripe? It was a momentous question. No more momentous question has been asked for a hundred years. The answer, so far, had been affirmative.

On this day, the 25th, from very early in the morning, the two corps marched south on each side of the great Forest of Mormal, the First Corps to the right and the Second to the left, as one faces the enemy. The position chosen for the next stand was in the neighbourhood of Le Cateau, on the line Cambrai-Le Cateau-Landrecies, and while the army was marching towards it, civilian labour was employed to prepare and entrench the ground. On this morning, also, the infantry of the Fourth Division, which had arrived at Le Cateau on the 23rd and 24th, became available for service, bringing a welcome addi-

On the Retreat from Mons

tion to our strength of eleven battalions. They were immediately sent forward, and, facing northwest between Solesmes and the Cambrai-Le Cateau road, materially assisted the retirement of the Second Corps. For both corps it was a day of terrible marching, along roads crowded with transport and—particularly on the eastern route—packed with refugees. For marching in a retreat has this fundamental disadvantage, that the men move behind their transport, and (in friendly country) with all the civilians of the countryside about their feet.

In such conditions a steady pace is the last thing to be hoped for. Checking—the curse of tired men—from being the exception becomes the rule; while the hours crawl on, and the boots tell, and the packs tell, and the eye grows glazed with staring at the men in front, and even the rifle, that "best friend," seems duller and heavier than a friend should be—the heaviest nine pounds in the world. It is calculated that on the 25th the various units of the Second Corps marched, under these most trying conditions, anything from twenty to thirty-five miles. By this time, also, the continual retirement was having its effect on the men's spirits. To the rank and file, who necessarily know nothing of high strategy, and see only what is before their eyes, the Retreat carried little of that high significance which we attach to it, but much of weariness and distaste.

Some glimmering of an idea that we were "leading the Germans into a trap" cheered men up here and there; some rumours of Russian victories raised the old jokes about "Berlin"; but for the most part they marched and fought uncomprehending, welcoming their turn of rear guard as a relief, because it gave some chance of fighting and turned their faces to the north.

The Second Corps reached their appointed line on the Cambrai-Le Cateau road as night was falling, and, under a cold, steady rain, which had succeeded the blazing heat of the day, proceeded to improve the trenches which they found there. They had had an exhausting march, but little fighting or interruption. The First Corps was delayed and did not reach the allotted position; but was scattered by the evening over an area at some points as many as thirty miles from the Second Corps, and nowhere nearer than Landrecies, eight miles from Le Cateau. The difficulty of movement had been increased by the convergence of French troops retiring from the Sambre, who cut across our line of march. The enemy pressure was continued by fresh troops well into the night. The engagement of the Second Division south and east of Maroilles, and the fight of the Fourth (Guards') Brigade at Landrecies, are the two main incidents in this difficult night's work.

About the fighting near Maroilles we have little information except that it seemed serious enough to justify the British commander-in-chief in asking for help from the French. In response to his urgent request two French reserve divisions attached to the Fifth French Army on our right eventually came up, and by diverting the attention of the enemy enabled Sir Douglas Haig to effect a skilful extrication from an awkward position made still more awkward by the darkness of night. One incident of the fighting near Maroilles has, indeed, slipped into the light of day with regard to a unit of the Second Division: a little rearguard action of the First Berks, near a bridge over the Petit Helpe which it was important to hold. They were on their way back to it, stumbling in the dark along a greasy, narrow causeway, with a deep ditch on each side, which led to the bridge.

> The Germans, as it turned out, had already forced the bridge and were in the act of advancing along the causeway; and in the pitch darkness of the night the two forces suddenly bumped one into the other. Neither side had fixed bayonets, for fear of accidents in the dark, and in the scrimmage which followed it was chiefly a case of rifle-butts and fists. At this game the Germans proved no match for our men, and were gradually forced back to the bridgehead, where they were held for the remainder of the night.

Early in the morning the Germans withdrew, and the First Berks fell back on the rest of the Second Division, along the road to Guise. It was a very complete and satisfactory little affair.

The fight at Landrecies by the Fourth (Guards') Brigade is better known. They had arrived there, very weary, and had got into billets; so weary, indeed, that the commander-in-chief could not order them farther west, to fill up the gap between Le Cateau and Landrecies. "The men were exhausted, and could not get farther in without rest." The enemy, however, would not allow them this rest. At 8.30 in the evening came news that Germans in motor-lorries were coming through the Forest of Mormal in great numbers, and bearing down upon the town. The town, fortunately, had already been put into a hasty state of defence: houses loop-holed, machineguns installed, barricades erected, and a company detailed to each of the many exits. It is said that the Germans advanced singing French songs, and that the leading ranks wore French uniforms, for a moment deceiving the defenders. This would explain

BATTLE OF MONS SURVIVORS RESTING

the suddenness of the collision, for the Germans and British were fighting hand to hand almost at once. It was a fierce fight while it lasted, and, with short respites, went on till the early hours of the morning; but eventually the enemy were beaten off with great loss.

It is estimated that they lost in this action from 700 to 1000 men. It must be allowed, nevertheless, in the light of later knowledge that the tactics of the Germans at Maroilles and Landrecies were good. A few battalions—for it is unlikely that they amounted to more—attacking at various points under cover of darkness with a great show of vigour, though beaten off, succeeded in conveying the impression to the British commanders in this part of the field that they were engaged with a considerable force. This impression once conveyed, the main object of the manoeuvre had been attained, for the First Corps was kept on the alert all night, and effectually prevented either from obtaining rest or from reaching its appointed destination in the British line. If our assumption of the enemy numbers is correct, it was a clever piece of work, well conceived and well executed.

The crisis of the Retreat was now approaching. There is a limit to what men can do, and it seemed for a moment as if this limit might be reached too soon. The commander-in-chief, seriously considering the accumulating strength of the enemy, the continued retirement of the French, his exposed left flank, the tendency of the enemy's western corps to envelop him, and above all, the exhausted and dispersed condition of his troops, decided to abandon the Le Cateau position, and to press on the Retreat till he could put some substantial obstacle, such as the Somme or the Oise, between his men and the enemy, behind which they might reorganize and rest. He therefore ordered his corps commanders to break off whatever action they might have in hand, and continue their retreat as soon as possible towards the new St. Quentin line.

The First Corps was by this time terribly exhausted, but, on receiving the order, set out from its scattered halting-places in the early hours of the 26th.

By dawn on that day the whole corps, including the Fourth Brigade at Landrecies, was moving south towards St. Quentin.

The order to retire at daybreak, on which the First Corps was now acting, had been duly received by the Second Corps. The commander had been informed that the retirement of the First Corps was to continue simultaneously and that three divisions of French cavalry under General Sordet were moving towards his left flank, in pursuance of

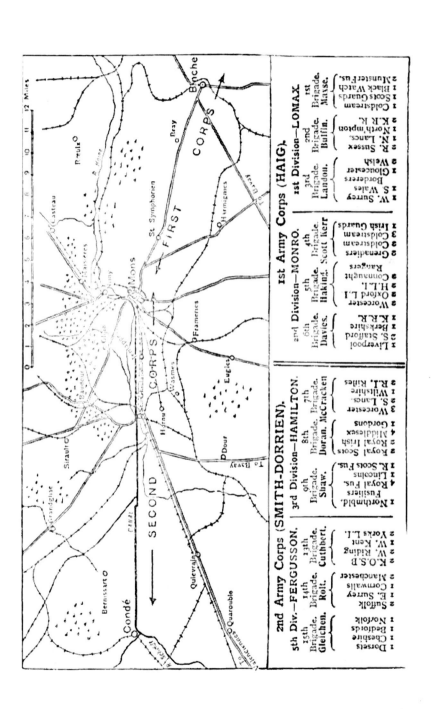

an agreement arrived at in a personal interview between the French cavalry commander and the British commander-in-chief.

Sir H. Smith-Dorrien was also informed that two French Territorial Divisions under General D'Amade were moving up to support Sordet.

There was no reason to suppose that the Second Corps, which had not been so much harassed by the enemy on its march south as the First Corps, was not equally well able to obey the order to retreat.

The corps commander, however, judged that his men were too tired and the enemy too strong to effect such a retirement as he was directed to carry out.

The general's reply was duly received at headquarters. The commander-in-chief was deeply engaged in concerting plans with the French commander-in-chief, his chief of the staff, and General Lanzerac (the commander of the Fifth French Army). Orders were immediately sent to the Second Corps, informing the general that any delay in retiring would seriously compromise the plan of the Allied operations, and, in view of the general situation, might entail fatal results. He was directed to resume his retirement forthwith, and, to assist him, the cavalry and Fourth Division were placed under his orders.

At the conclusion of the conference, no positive information having been received of the commencement of the retirement, the commander-in-chief himself set out for Le Cateau[1]; but the congestion of the roads with Belgian refugees, etc., made progress so slow that he had not accomplished half the distance before he found that his orders had been carried out and the retirement was in progress.

During the early part of the day, however, Sir H. Smith-Dorrien had, for the reason given above, waited at the Le Cateau position to engage the pursuing Germans. Of the three divisions of infantry thus engaged, the Fifth lay on the right, the Third in the centre, and the Fourth faced outwards on the left: the whole occupying the ridge south of the Cambrai-Le Cateau road, on the line Haucourt-Caudry-Beaumont-Le Cateau. The Nineteenth Infantry Brigade was in reserve and the cavalry operated on the flanks. With both flanks exposed, with three divisions of infantry to the enemy's seven, and faced by the massed artillery of four army corps,—an odds of four or five to one,—the Second Corps and Fourth Division prepared to

---

1. *Guns at Le Cateau*, Two Accounts of the B.E.F. in the First World War, *The Royal Regiment of Artillery at Le Cateau*, 26 August, 1914 by A. F. Becke and *The Stand at Le Cateau, 26th August, 1914* by C. de Sausmarez is also published by Leonaur.

make a stand. A few hours' sleep, and at dawn, with a roar of guns, the battle opened.

That the day was critical, that it was all or nothing, was realised by all ranks. Everything was thrown into the scale; nothing was held back. Regiments and batteries, with complete self-abandonment, faced hopeless duels at impossible ranges; brigades of cavalry on the flanks boldly threatened divisions; and in the half-shelter of their trenches the infantry, withering but never budging, grimly dwindled before the German guns. It was our first experience on a large scale of modern artillery in mass. For the first six hours the guns never stopped. To our infantry it was a time of stubborn and almost stupefied endurance, broken by lucid intervals of that deadly musketry which had played such havoc with the Germans at Mons. To our artillery it was a duel, and perhaps of all the displays of constancy and devotion in a battle where every man in every arm of the service did his best, the display of the gunners was the finest. For they accepted the duel quite cheer-fully, and made such sport with the enemy's infantry that even their masses shivered and recoiled. By midday, however, many of our bat-teries were out of action, and the enemy infantry had advanced almost to the main Cambrai-Le Cateau road, behind which our men, in their pathetic civilian trenches, were quietly waiting.

The enemy attacked on the right of the Fifth Division, and were in the act of turning it when the order came to retire. This necessary order, for a gradual retirement from the right, was issued a little before 3 p.m., and was with great difficulty conveyed to all parts of the line. In the Fifth Division several companies, in covering the retirement, were practically wiped out. The story of "B" Company of the Sec-ond K.O.Y.L.I. charging the enemy with its nineteen remaining men, headed by its commander, is typical of the spirit which inspired the British regiments.

The Third Division had suffered comparatively little when the order reached them, and were justly priding themselves on having successfully repulsed a determined attack on Caudry, the apex of the position.

On the left of the line was posted the Fourth Division which had come in by train the previous day, and was personally placed by the commander-in-chief in the position he thought best to cover the re-tirement of the Second Corps.

Owing to the unexpected turn of events at Mons, and the unfor-tunate delay in the despatch of this division from England, the troops had to be pushed into action without a moment's delay, and before the detrainment of their artillery and other services was practically complete.

On the morning of the 26th they found themselves on the extreme western flank of the Allied forces, and splendidly did General Snow and his gallant men carry out the difficult and dangerous task assigned them.

The conduct of their retirement was no less efficient than their gallant fighting. Parts of this division, however, shared the fate of other units in the line engaged in covering the retirement, and, holding on into the night, either retired in the darkness (some to the British lines, others through the German lines to the sea) or, less fortunate, were cut off, captured, or destroyed. Many adventures befell them, and some tragedies, but none to equal the tragedy of the First Gordons, who marched in the darkness into a German division in bivouac some miles south of the battleground, and were shot or taken prisoners almost to a man.

The infantry retirement, though thus partial and irregular, was progressively carried out according to orders, and by four o'clock in the afternoon most of the line had been cleared. The retirement was covered by the artillery, still in action with the same unruffled courage and devotion which they had shown throughout the day, and there is no doubt that the reluctance of the enemy to engage in an energetic pursuit was partly due to this splendid opposition of our gunners, as well as to the undoubtedly heavy losses which they had suffered from our rifle and shell fire earlier in the day. At any rate, the pursuit was not pressed, and by nightfall, after another long and weary march,—how weary, after such a day, can scarcely be expressed,—the remains of the Second Corps and the Fourth Division halted and bivouacked. It was pouring with rain, but many slept where they halted, by the roadside, too utterly worn to think of shelter.

There is a pendant to this great action of the 26th which until recently has been missing from its place; and it has been a matter of much wonder, in consequence, how it was that things fell out as they did after the Battle of Le Cateau, the weary British retiring before a numerous and victorious enemy which did not pursue. It was pointed out, indeed, that the enemy had suffered heavy losses; that they were tired and shaken by the unexpected violence of the British defence; but when every allowance had been made for the effect of weariness and loss, it was plain that some other reason must still be found to account for a decision so repugnant to the German temper and the German plans. Reference has already been made to the promise made by Generals Sordet and D'Amade to the British Commander-in-Chief. If history has been slow to record it, let the delay be put down to the exigencies of war. The enemy were not only tired and shaken. They were also threatened, and threatened, as they very quickly discovered, in the most sensitive tentacles of their advance.

It was about 4.30 on the afternoon of the 26th (so the story runs), when the British retirement had been in progress about an hour, that a furious cannonading was heard out towards the west. This was Sordet's cavalry, tired horses and all, arrived and engaging the German right. The explanation was confirmed by airmen later in the day, who reported having seen large bodies of French cavalry, with horse artillery and some battalions of infantry, driving back the Germans out towards Cambrai. General Sordet and his cavalry, aided by General D'Amade's battalions, which had moved out from their station at Arras, were able to inflict upon the outflanking German right a blow which recoiled upon the whole of the First German Army, and by its threatened significance more than by its actual strength dominated the policy of that army for several days to come. The German advance wavered and paused, and for nearly twenty-four hours the British continued their retirement almost unmolested.

Whether on the early morning of the 26th the left of the British line could have followed the example of the First Corps and continued its retreat, is a question which cannot be satisfactorily settled until the whole history of the war is laid bare. But there can be no doubt that both troops and commander richly deserved the high tribute paid them in the despatch of the British commander-in-chief, who, after praising the behaviour of various arms, says:—

I cannot close this brief account of the glorious stand of the British troops without putting on record my deep appreciation of the valuable services rendered by Sir H. Smith-Dorrien.
I say without hesitation that the saving of the left wing of the army under my command on the morning of the 26th August could never have been accomplished unless a commander of rare and unusual coolness, intrepidity, and determination had been present to personally conduct the operations.

It is impossible to close the story of this, the most critical time of the great Retreat, without making mention of the inestimable services performed by the British cavalry under General Allenby. The moral superiority which they had so effectually established over the hostile horsemen during the enemy's first advance on Mons, was maintained and increased by every one of the many trials of strength which occurred all along the line between smaller and greater units of the two opposing cavalries. Invariably in all these encounters the German cavalry were driven behind the protection of their infantry and, thus hampering the latter's advance, assisted our troops to make good their retreat. The quality of the horses and equipment of the British, their unrivalled efficiency in dismounted fighting and in knowledge of ground, coupled with their intrepidity and dash whenever the smallest opportunity for mounted attack presented itself, enabled them effectually to prevent that which is most dreaded by a retreating army—the enterprises of hostile horsemen.

No praise can be too great for the British cavalry throughout this drastic initiation into the splendid work which they have invariably performed throughout the campaign.

It was in the early hours of the morning of the 27th that the commander of the Second Corps personally reported himself at headquarters. He informed the commander-in-chief that the Second Corps and Fourth Division had suffered heavily and were very tired, but were now rapidly regaining order and cohesion. By dawn every available staff officer was *en route* for St. Quentin, and hour after hour, at their posts on the line of the Retreat, shepherded the troops towards their units, and the longed-for luxuries of food and drink and news. All through the morning detachments of every size and every conceivable composition kept filing past—some with officers, most with none—some hobbling and silent, others whistling and in step—but all with one accord most thoroughly persuaded (such are the fallacies of a retreat) that they were the last and only survivors of their respective commands. Many, after a brief halt, had marched all night, and up to one o'clock in the afternoon they were still coming in. A brief rest, some bread and coffee, and they were off once more, their troubles almost forgotten in the pleasure of rejoining their regiments and recovering their friends.

The general Retreat, which the Battle of Le Cateau had so dangerously interrupted, resumed once more its normal tenor. Of the behaviour of the men during this trying period it is difficult to speak with moderation. They had passed through an ordeal, both physical and mental, such as few troops have ever had to face in their first week of war; and had displayed throughout a nobility of bearing and demeanour of which none who observed them can speak even now without emotion. Such courage and patience, such humorous resignation and cheerfulness in adversity, are to be paralleled only in the finest armies of history.

The resumption of the general Retreat and the restoration of march routine among the forces of the British left had one immediate and important consequence. It became possible to deal with the chief remaining weakness caused by the inability of the First Corps, as already pointed out, to reach its allotted position on the evening of the 25th. The First Corps had not been idle while the Second Corps fought; though never heavily engaged, it had been perpetually harassed, and was still, on August 27, suffering from the wide dispersion of its forces on the 25th. It was now moving south as best it could—keeping direction, but otherwise marching and bivouacking by brigades. On both flanks, indeed, throughout these early days of the Retreat, such was the imminence of the enemy, and such the variety of fortunes of the different brigades—and even battalions and companies—of the same division during any one day, that no strict uniformity of march or of line could be looked for.

It speaks well for the commanders of brigade and regimental units that so unusually high a discretionary power was exercised so well, and with so little miscarriage either of individual units or of the general scheme. Some mishaps, of course, there were, of companies and battalions overtaken, cut off, or surprised. The capture of the greater part of the Second Munster Fusiliers at Bergues on the 26th is one of these incidents, to be set beside the destruction of the First Gordons, as part of the tragic waste inevitable in any continuous retreat before superior numbers. It is memorable, not only because, like the First Gordons, the regiment involved carried a famous name, but because it gave occasion to our cavalry to show once more in their Retreat their devotion to duty. It was entirely due to the skilful and audacious dismounted action of two troops of the Fifteenth Hussars that the battered remnant of the Munsters—about one hundred and fifty men—was saved from annihilation or surrender.

The Second Corps was still, on August 27, in advance of the First; but in both corps the Retreat continued incessantly. Sleep was cut down to a minimum; men fed, drank, and slept as they could, and always, when they rose from the roadside and stretched themselves to a new dawn, the word was "March." Their chief enemy now was not the Germans, but the road, the blazing sun, and the limits of their own flesh and blood. The worst, however, was over. By August 27/28 movement by divisions began to be possible; and by August 28 movement by corps. By August 28/29 the whole army was in touch once more on the line Noyon-La Fère, and on Sunday the 29th, for the first time for eight days, the army actually rested. It is a day they are never likely to forget. While the men rested, their commanders took stock; and before the march was resumed, brigades and divisions had been reorganised, stragglers restored, and deficiencies of men and material ascertained and noted. The reorganisation was completed by the arrival of Major-General Pulteney, and the constitution of the Fourth Division and Nineteenth Infantry Brigade as a Third Army Corps under his command.

The reorganisation of the British Force coincided with a gratifying change in the Allied dispositions. The British Army was not only in touch within itself, but in touch, also, on both its flanks, with the French; on the right, with the Fifth French Army, now, after many vicissitudes and much hard fighting, lying behind the Oise from La Fère to Guise; and on the left with a new French Army, still in process of formation, of which the nucleus was those same two divisions of infantry and three divisions of cavalry which General D'Amade and General Sordet had handled so much to our advantage on the afternoon of the 26th, and throughout the subsequent retirement. This army (to be called henceforth, the Sixth) conscious of some mission above the ordinary, and daily increasing in strength, lay off, on the 29th, to the northwest of the British line, facing northeast with its right on Roye.

It was a welcome change, removing none too soon that fear of isolation which had haunted all our movements. The situation of the British, scars and bruises notwithstanding, seemed suddenly almost promising, and with their flanks secured, for the first time since the Retreat began, they enjoyed a genuine feeling of relaxation. It was a feeling, happily, which the enemy at the moment was unable to disturb. His strength was diverted to the two French Armies, and except for some cavalry actions, in which our troops as usual were completely successful, there was little activity on the British front. On the morning of the 29th, while our men were resting behind the Oise, the main body of the pursuit was still engaged in crossing the Somme.

It was amazing to see how quickly the army recovered during these days from the first strain of the Retreat. Even on the 28th the improvement was notable. A general cheerfulness pervaded the ranks, whence derived no one seemed to care, but splendid and infectious. Men toughened and hardened; the limpers grew fewer, and already battalions were to be met marching with the old swing to the old song. By the 29th—for always we come back to this crucial date—the first hard apprenticeship was over; and when the army rose from its sleep to take the road once more, it looked and felt an army of veterans. Officers smiled as they watched their men, and speculated happily on the day to come.

The chief difficulty now was to replace wastage in equipment, etc., which had been enormous. For in the strain and confusion of the Retreat everything detachable had been lost or thrown away, and whole companies were found, perfectly fitted out eight days before, which had now scarcely a single greatcoat, waterproof sheet, or change of clothing left. The deficiency of entrenching tools—to take only one article of equipment, though that, perhaps, the most easily lost—amounted, in the troops which had fought at Le Cateau, to over eighty per cent. It was much easier, unfortunately, to tabulate these deficiencies than to supply them. The stores existed, indeed, but they were not to be had. They were lying for the fetching on the quays and in the depots of Havre and Rouen and Boulogne, but every day's march took us farther away from them and increased their exposure to the German advance.

With Amiens already in the enemy's hands, and the Channel ports uncovered, we were, for a moment, that portent of the textbooks, an army without a base. It was a case for prompt measures, and prompt measures were taken. On August 29, while the army was recounting deficiencies on the Oise, the inspector general of the lines of communication, by order of the commander-in-chief, was arranging a grand removal to the mouth of the Loire, and on August 30, the new British base was temporarily established at St. Nazaire and Nantes, with Le Mans as advanced base in place of Amiens. It was a great achievement, but an unwelcome change, for both by sea and by land the distances were greater, and it had the inevitable consequence of delaying the arrival of everything on which the army depended for replenishment. The infantry went without their greatcoats and entrenching tools; and though reinforcements of men continued to arrive at stated intervals,—the first reinforcement on September 5, and the second on September 7 and 8,—the guns which should have come on August 29 were not actually received till September 19. It was not until October 11, when the British Army was setting out for Flanders, that St. Nazaire was at last definitely closed down, and Havre and Boulogne reopened in its place. It was a difficult period for the administrative departments of the army, and had its own triumphs.

The lull in operations on the British front during the 29th, and the restoration of contact with the French, were turned to good account by the Allied leaders, whose opportunities for meeting and exchanging views had hitherto been rare. A conference was held in the early afternoon at British Headquarters in Compiègne, which was attended not only by General Joffre and Sir John French, but by the three British corps commanders and General Allenby. The conference was presided over by the French commander-in-chief, who showed himself, then as always, where the British were concerned, "most kind, cordial, and sympathetic." Sir John French says:

> He told me that he had directed the Fifth French Army on the Oise to move forward and attack the Germans on the Somme, with a view to checking pursuit. He also told me of the formation of the Sixth French Army on my left flank, composed of the Seventh Army Corps, four reserve divisions, and Sordet's corps of cavalry.

In conclusion, having dealt with the immediate necessities of the British, he outlined once more his strategic conception, to draw on the enemy at all points until a favourable situation should be created for the desired offensive, and in conformity with that conception directed the Retreat to proceed. The bridges over the Oise were promptly destroyed, and at various hours between mid-afternoon of the 29th and early morning of the 30th the British forces set out on a twenty-mile march to the Aisne, through beautiful country which they were no longer too tired to enjoy. By the afternoon of August 30, the whole army was in position a few miles north of the line Compiègne-Soissons, and at the same time the Germans occupied La Fère. On the morning of August 31 the Retreat was resumed, and from this date until September 4 continued practically from day to day in conformity with the movements of the French, our men becoming daily fitter and more war-hardened. Rumours, however, of successful French actions on our flanks, and, amidst much that was vague and wearisome, a growing sense of combination and ulterior purpose in their movements, encouraged all ranks.

The country now was much more difficult, for after the Forest of

Compiègne is passed the land plunges into deep wooded ravines and break-neck roads, very trying for guns and transport, and for all manner of manoeuvres. The heat was intense, and, to make matters worse, the enemy pursuit, which had unaccountably languished, was becoming closer and more insistent. The British, bivouacked that night between Crépy-en-Valois and Villers-Cotteret, found themselves committed, on the morning of September 1, to two of the hottest skirmishes of the Retreat; one at Villers-Cotteret, where the Fourth (Guards') Brigade was covering the retirement of the Second Division, the other on the left at Néry, in the area of the Third Corps.

The action at Villers-Cotteret began about nine o'clock, in very difficult forest country, and continued until after midday, the Guards' Brigade maintaining its ground, despite heavy losses, with a steadiness and determination worthy of the heroes of Landrecies. It was an action easily described. The attack had been expected, and was repulsed. In this action the Irish Guards, who had only been under distant shell fire at Mons and had had little to do at Landrecies, received their full baptism of fire. It was their first real fight, and their commanding officer headed the casualty list. The action at Néry was quite unlike the action at Villers-Cotteret, for it came as a surprise, and at one time looked like becoming a tragedy.

The first indication of danger had reached the headquarters of the Second Corps at three o'clock in the morning, when a Frenchman reported having seen "forty German guns and a large force of *Uhlans*" moving in the direction of the Third Corps, and more particularly in the direction of Néry, where the First Cavalry Brigade with L Battery, R.H.A., was billeted, on the left front of the British line. Except as regards the number of the guns the report proved to be true. The Germans, concealed from the British by a thick mist,—six regiments of cavalry with two batteries of six guns each,—were in position by daybreak on the steep ridge which overlooks the village, when an officer's patrol of the Eleventh Hussars bumped suddenly into them out of the mist. It is possible that they were as much surprised as the British, for a mist works both ways; but they had the advantage in numbers, armament, and position. The alarm was scarcely given when their guns opened on the village, and by five o'clock, when the sun rose, the fight was in full swing.

It was a singular action, for though our cavalry, dismounted and hastily disposed, soon recovered from their surprise, nothing could alter the situation of L Battery. Thanks to the mist, it had been caught in a position as unsuitable for action as could well be conceived. Un-limbered in an orchard only four hundred yards off, and perfectly commanded by the German guns, it was throughout the fight a mere target for the enemy. A tornado of shell, machine-gun, and rifle fire was directed upon it, the battery meanwhile boldly replying, though its case was hopeless, and known to be hopeless, from the first. Soon only one of its guns was left in action, and on the serving of this one gun the attention of every surviving officer and man was concentrated, one after another falling killed or wounded under the fire of the now exasperated enemy. Captain Bradbury, loading, lost a leg; continued to direct, and lost the other, and was carried away to die so that, as he said, his men should not see his agony and be discouraged.

When all the officers had fallen, Sergeant-Major Dorrell took command, and aided by the machine-guns of the Eleventh Hussars, was still maintaining the hopeless duel when about eight o'clock the Fourth Cavalry Brigade arrived, and not long after the First Middlesex leading the Nineteenth Infantry Brigade. The balance was reversed, and the enemy, with, it is said, the one gun of L Battery still firing at them, retired in disorder towards Verrines, leaving eight of their twelve guns on the field. Whatever their mission, it remained unfulfilled. In this action, in which a serious disaster was so successfully averted, the heroic performance of L Battery will always be memorable. It had lost, during the engagement, all its officers and eighty *per cent* of its gun detachments killed or wounded, without betraying by so much as a sign either discouragement or defeat. Distinctions were showered upon it, and Captain Bradbury, Sergeant-Major Dorrell, and Sergeant Nelson were awarded the Victoria Cross.

There is a sequel to this fight too exhilarating to be omitted. As the First and Fourth Cavalry Brigades were moving south next morning through the rides of the Forest of Ermenonville, they came on the tracks of horses and sent a troop to follow them up.

They found the ride strewn with German kit of all kinds, lame horses, etc., showing a hurried retreat. They had gone by five hours before, and turned out to be our Néry friends, the cavalry division, who had bumped into one of our columns and retreated rapidly, leaving their four remaining guns.

It was a very satisfactory finish, and had a fine effect on the whole army. The story of the capture of the twelve guns ran like wildfire through the ranks, and was recorded with pleasure by the French in their communiqué.

On September 2, very early in the morning, the army was once more on the move. September 1 had been a hard day, and at one time something like a general engagement was threatened on the left and left centre of the British line, the Fifth and Fourth Divisions fighting model rear-guard actions which had much to do with the inactivity of the enemy on the following day. For on September 2 the pursuit once more relaxed, and by the evening the British had reached the north bank of the Marne, and were already arranging for the crossing on the following day. Both the march and the crossing had been contemplated with considerable misgiving by the commander-in-chief, for on September 2 the army was no longer retiring, as it had hitherto retired, in the direction of Paris, but, owing to the position of the bridges, had swung southeast and was now executing what was in effect almost a flank march in the face of the enemy.

The crossing of the Marne was an even more delicate operation, for it involved, in circumstances of comparative immobility, the same dangerous exposure to the enemy. The enemy, however, did nothing to interrupt our operations, and was, indeed, reported by our airmen to have swung southeast also, and to be moving in the direction of Château-Thierry, towards the front of the Fifth French Army. By the night of September 3 the whole of the British troops were safely across the river and all the bridges blown up. The left of the British Army was now actually in sight of the outlying forts of Paris, and there was much excitement among all ranks as to our ultimate destination. Should we, after all, enter Paris, and sleep in the beds of *la ville lumière*? It was not to be. A position was occupied between Lagny and Signy-Signets, and on the following day, while the enemy was bridging the Marne, the British Army made the last stage of the Retreat, finishing up, in the cool of the evening, on the line Lagny-Courtagon. This was their "farthest south," and on September 5, while they rested, the great news spread through the army that the Retreat was over, and that next day the Advance would begin.

It would be difficult to exaggerate the effect of the news. For though the army had grown outwardly fitter and more cheerful during the last seven days, the profound distaste which was felt by all ranks for the perpetual retirement poisoned every activity. Was it never to end, this Retreat? Were we retiring, then, to the Pyrenees? With such bitter questions and mock-humorous answers, they beguiled the march. When the news came it was as if a great sickness had been lifted from their minds, and for the first time, perhaps, they realised fully, as men do when they rise from sickness, how infinitely tired and weary they had been. They could scarcely believe the news; but it came from quarters not to be denied. The "favourable situation" for which General Joffre had been waiting so patiently had come at last.

The Fighting Retreat to Paris

Contents

CHAPTER 1

The King's Message to His Troops

By the middle of the third week of the war, the British Expeditionary Force—three army corps and a cavalry division—had been mobilised and sent across the Channel to France. Sir John French's force was the largest army that England had ever sent into the field at the outset of a campaign. Its mobilisation, concentration, and transport across the narrow seas had been carried out with silent efficiency. England waited confidently and patiently for the tidings of its entry into the battle line.

On August 9 the king had issued to his troops on their departure for the front the following message:—

> Buckingham Palace,
> Aug, 9, 1914.
>
> You are leaving home to fight for the safety and honour of my Empire.
>
> Belgium, whose country we are pledged to defend, has been attacked, and France is about to be invaded by the same powerful foe.
>
> I have implicit confidence in you, my soldiers. Duty is your watchword, and I know your duty will be nobly done.
>
> I shall follow your every movement with deepest interest, and mark with eager satisfaction your daily progress; indeed, your welfare will never be absent from my thoughts.
>
> I pray God to bless you and guard you and bring you back victorious.
>
> George R.I.

Lord Kitchener also addressed to the forces these instructions, to be kept in the Active Service Pay-book of every soldier in the Expe-

51

BRITISH EXPEDITIONARY FORCE DISEMBARKING AT BOULOGNE AND BRIT-
ISH ARTILLERY AND GUNS PASSING THROUGH BOULOGNE.

ditionary army:

> You are ordered abroad as a soldier of the king to help our French comrades against the invasion of a common enemy. You have to perform a task which will need your courage, your energy, your patience. Remember that the honour of the British Army depends on your individual conduct. It will be your duty not only to set an example of discipline and perfect steadiness under fire, but also to maintain the most friendly relations with those whom you are helping in this struggle.
>
> The operations in which you are engaged will, for the most part, take place in a friendly country, and you can do your own country no better service than in showing yourselves in France and Belgium in the true character of a British soldier.
>
> Be invariably courteous, considerate, and kind. Never do anything likely to injure or destroy property, and always look upon looting as a disgraceful act. You are sure to meet with a welcome and to be trusted; your conduct must justify that welcome and that trust. Your duty cannot be done unless your health is sound. So keep constantly on your guard against any excesses. In this new experience you may find temptations both in wine and women. You must entirely resist both temptations, and, while treating all women with perfect courtesy, you should avoid any intimacy.
>
> > Do your duty bravely.
> > Fear God,
> > Honour the King.
>
> (Signed)   Kitchener, Field Marshal.

On the day before the Expeditionary Forces were announced to have landed safely in France, the British Army sustained a severe loss through the sudden death, on August 17, of Lieut.-General Sir James Moncrieff Grierson. This brilliant and accomplished soldier, who was to have commanded the Second Corps (third and fifth divisions), was succeeded by General Sir Horace Smith-Dorrien. The First Corps (first and second divisions) was commanded by Lieut.-General Sir Douglas Haig, the Third Corps (fourth and sixth divisions) by Major-General W. P. Pulteney, and Major-General Edmund Allenby was in command of the cavalry division.

After the lapse of nearly a hundred years, then, the British troops found themselves once more on Belgian soil with a heavy task in front of them. As in 1815, the object of the Allies was to liberate Europe from the domination of a military despot. In the present conflict the Prussians, whom we had so often supported on the field, were against us, while we were ranged on the side of our old foes at Waterloo.

Our forces were placed on the left of the line on which the Allied armies advanced to the help of Belgium. Liège had fallen, but Namur was holding out. The plan of campaign was that of the French staff, under the command of General Joffre, and was based on the general idea of a march across the Belgian frontier on the west of the Meuse with the left towards Tournai. It was expected that, after a first battle with the German Army in Belgium near the border, the enemy would be driven back to the northeast, hands would be joined with the heroic Belgian Army, Brussels abandoned by the invaders, and the siege of Namur raised.

Sir John French issued a stirring "order of the day" to the British Expedition at the moment, when our forces were complete, and our columns formed for advance. In the course of "a few brief words to the officers, non-commissioned officers, and men I have the honour and the privilege to command," the commander-in-chief said:—

> Our cause is just. We are called upon to fight beside our gallant Allies in France and Belgium in no war of arrogance, but to uphold our national honour, independence, and freedom.
> I have in peace time repeatedly pointed out to you that the strength and efficiency of a modern army in the field is to be measured more by the amount of individual intelligence which permeates throughout its ranks than by its actual numbers.
> In peace time your officers and non-commissioned officers have striven hard to cultivate this intelligence and power of initiative. I call upon you individually to use your utmost endeavour to profit by this training and instruction. Have confidence in yourselves, and in the knowledge of your powers.
> Having, then, this trust in the righteousness of our cause, pride in the glory of our military traditions, and belief in the efficiency of our army, we go forward to do or die for God, King, and Country.

The disposition of the French forces was described by a statement issued from the War Office at Paris as follows:—

> An army starting out from the Wavre in the north, and going in the direction of Neufchâteau, is attacking the German

troops which have been pouring down the Grand Duchy of Luxemburg along the western bank of the Semoy, and going in a Westerly direction.

Another army which left from the region of Sedan and crossed the Ardennes is attacking several German army corps that were on the march between the Lesse and the Meuse.

A third army from the region of Chimay has been moved forward to make an attack on the German right between the Sambre and the Meuse, and is supported by the English army which set out from the region of Mons.

The movement of the Germans who had sought to envelop our left wing has been followed step by step, and their right is now being attacked by our army forming our left wing, in junction with the English Army. At this point the battle has been raging violently for more than a day.

The Germans had concentrated a huge mass of men for the attack on the left of the allied lines, held by the British troops, with the object of dealing them a smashing blow and of forcing their way south. They were determined to carry out the Army Orders of August 19 in which the German emperor declared with characteristic assurance that:—

> It is my Royal and Imperial Command that you concentrate your energies, for the immediate present, upon one single purpose, and that is that you address all your skill and all the valour of my soldiers to exterminate first the treacherous English and walk over General French's contemptible little army.
>
> Headquarters,
> Aix-la-Chapelle.

Men and guns were not wanting for this assault. The shrapnel was deadly in its effect, but the marksmanship of the German rifles is stated to have been uniformly poor. To make assurance doubly sure, the troops pitted against our men were some of the best, as testified by the statement of a wounded Belfast man:—

> You must remember that for almost twenty-four hours we bore the brunt of the attack, and the desperate fury with which the Germans fought showed that they believed if they were only once past the British forces the rest would be easy. Not only so, but I am sure we had the finest troops in the German Army

55

Getting forward with the guns.

French soldiers of the Line watching the arrival of their British allies.

A halt by the wayside.

against us.

On the way out I had heard some slighting comments passed on the German troops, and no doubt some of them are not worth much, but those thrown at us were very fine specimens indeed. I do not think they could have been beaten in that respect.

Mr. William Maxwell wrote, on August 21, from Mons:—

It was like a great river bursting its banks. The moment the Belgians were forced to retire to their entrenched camp at Antwerp, the Germans swept over the country without check west toward Ghent, south toward Mons. The enemy was committed to a great turning movement. It was striving to hold the French along the Meuse between Namur and Dinant, while its armies west of the river were marching south along a front of many miles. One army threatens Mons with the object of penetrating the French frontier and descending on Maubeuge and Valenciennes, another army was advancing toward the line of Tournai—Coutrai which covers the great city of Lille. At Ath there were indications that the enemy was advancing south along the Enghien—Soignies, though he seemed to avoid the main road at Jurbise. By deserted country paths from this point I came to Mons.

Here as everywhere great fear was manifested by the citizens at the approach of the *Uhlans*. The authorities had been warned by telephone that they were near.

They pretend that they are English and then when the villagers cry '*Vive l'Angleterre*,' they find out their mistake.

On the same day, a French witness, the correspondent of a Paris paper, spoke of the German advance as extending:

. . . . over a line of nearly 100 miles, spreading out in a formidable fan-like movement, preceded by a swarm of scouts in all directions, which sweeps over the country from Brussels to Arlon. The German hordes are on the march over five different routes towards France. They will find men to meet them.

M. Auguste Mellot, deputy of Namur, saw in that town on August 21 eleven German Army Corps "pass the Meuse coming from Visé, a powerful force being detailed to mask their march." The German troops engaged in this action probably amounted to fewer than half that number.

The lines of the Allied armies practically covered every assailable point from Condé to Dinant. Mr. Maxwell thus described the position of the British forces just before the great battle which began on Saturday, August 22:—

The 1st British Cavalry Division (General Allenby) had its headquarters at Givry, close to the frontier, and was moving north in the direction of Binche. Cavalry covered the south-east of Mons. It was pushed forward also toward Fontaine l'Évêque, west of Charleroi, and, generally speaking, threatened to raid the left flank of the Germans advancing rapidly from the direction of Brussels.

An immense army was gathered on the frontier, and had passed into Belgium. Mons was the point of greatest concentration of the British. It was an army marching to attack, for there was no attempt at making defensive works. From Mons the British army extended west along the canal from Mons, from Maubeuge through Bavay, on to Valenciennes, where the Highland regiments created immense enthusiasm. From the western end of the canal at Mons, Belgian territory has few defenders. Most of the men have been withdrawn from that side. Prussian patrols swarm over the country, and it is clear that behind them is a great army.

Sir John French, in his first admirable despatch, gives a history of the activities of the British Expeditionary Force during that eventful week in August from the 21st to the 28th when our troops were fighting against overwhelming odds. We will divide the despatch into sections, which will fall into place as our story proceeds. He says:—

The concentration (of the troops) was practically complete on the evening of Friday, August the 21st, and I was able to make dispositions to move the force during Saturday, the 22nd, to positions I considered most favourable from which to commence operations which the French commander-in-chief, General Joffre, requested me to undertake in pursuance of his plans in the prosecution of the campaign.

The line taken up extended along the line of the canal from Condé on the west, through Mons and Binche on the east. This line was taken up as follows:—

From Condé to Mons inclusive was assigned to the Second Corps, and to the right of the Second Corps from Mons the First Corps was posted. The 5th Cavalry Brigade was placed at Binche.

In the absence of my Third Army Corps I desired to keep the cavalry division as much as possible as a reserve to act on my outer flank, or move in support of any threatened part of the line. The forward reconnaissance was entrusted to Brigadier-General Sir Philip Chetwode with the 5th Cavalry Brigade, but I directed General Allenby to send forward a few squadrons to assist in this work.

During the 22nd and 23rd these advanced squadrons did some excellent work, some of them penetrating as far as Soignies, and several encounters took place in which our troops showed to great advantage.

The scouting operations of the British cavalry extended south-westward of Brussels and south-east as far as Charleroi. The German cavalry were well-nigh exhausted by their ceaseless exertions, but a rapid advance was necessary for their success, and it was clear that they would proceed without delay; while our cavalry scoured the country for any signs of the German advance. The French were coming up from the south. A wounded soldier in the British hussars stated that on Friday, August 21, his party encountered some of the 4th Cuirassiers. The two forces without any warning came face to face round the turn of a small village street. They immediately attacked one another as quickly as their horses could move, much to the alarm of the village people, who made for their houses, screaming with terror. It was a genuine cavalry charge without the discharge of a gun. The hussars were the lighter, consequently they had the advantage as regards speed, for the horses of the *cuirassiers* were dead beat. The result of the encounter was 27 Germans killed and 12 taken prisoners.

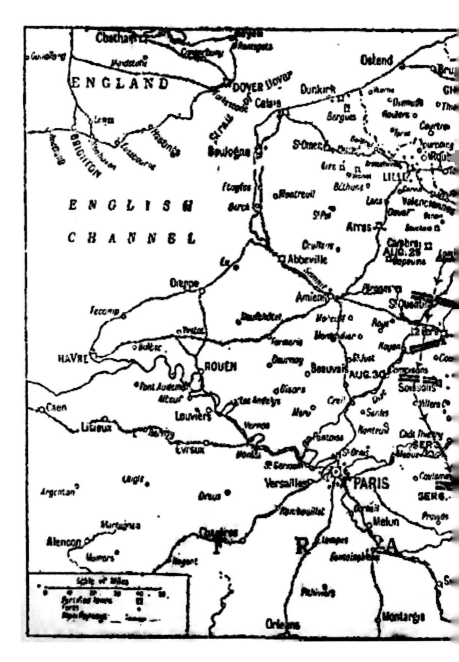

POSITION OF THE BRITISH FORCE

IN THE RETREAT TOWARDS PARIS

CHAPTER 2

The Battle of Mons, August 23rd

In the following section of Sir John French's despatch he describes the position on Sunday, August 23:—

At 6 a.m. on August 23 I assembled the commanders of the First and Second Corps and Cavalry Division at a point close to the position, and explained the general situation of the Allies, and what I understood to be General Joffre's plan. I discussed with them at some length the immediate situation in front of us.

From information I received from French Headquarters I understood that little more than one, or at most two, of the enemy's army corps, with perhaps one cavalry division, were in front of my position; and I was aware of no attempted outflanking movement by the enemy. I was confirmed in this opinion by the fact that my patrols encountered no undue opposition in their reconnoitring operations. The observation of my aeroplanes seemed also to bear out this estimate.

About 3 p.m. on Sunday, the 23rd, reports began coming in to the effect that the enemy was commencing an attack on the Mons line, apparently in some strength, but that the right of the position from Mons and Bray was being particularly threatened.

The commander of the First Corps had pushed his flank back to some high ground south of Bray, and the 5th Cavalry Brigade evacuated Binche, moving slightly south; the enemy thereupon occupied Binche.

The right of the 3rd Division, under General Hamilton, was at Mons, which formed a somewhat dangerous salient; and I directed the commander of the Second Corps to be careful not to keep the troops on this salient too long, but, if threatened seriously, to draw back the centre behind Mons. This was done before dark. In the meantime, about 5 p.m., I received a most unexpected message from General Joffre by telegraph, telling me that at least three German Corps, *viz.*, a reserve corps, the 4th Corps, and the 9th Corps, were moving on my position in front, and that the Second Corps was engaged in a turning movement from the direction of Tournai. He also informed me that two reserve French divisions and the 5th French Army on my right were retiring, the Germans having on the previous day gained possession of the passages of the Sambre between Charleroi and Namur.

An official statement issued by the Press Bureau announced that the British troops took an active and meritorious part in the great battle which began on Saturday, August 22. Throughout an engagement on Sunday near Mons they held their ground, and they had successfully reached their new position. Fighting had gone on more or less continuously, but the enemy had not harassed our operations and the movement was executed with great skill by the commanders of the First and Second Army Corps. Casualties could not be estimated exactly, but were not heavy. Our forces were opposed by two German army corps and two cavalry divisions. The enemy suffered very heavily. The position now occupied was well protected.

The general position showed that the Allies continued the action in Belgium on Sunday and Monday, August 23 and 24, but in presence of the considerable forces which the Germans had massed the French commander-in-chief decided to withdraw his troops to the original line of defence arranged, where they were firmly established. Two French divisions suffered somewhat severely, but the main body was not touched and remained full of enthusiasm. The German losses, particularly in the *corps d'armée* of the Guards, were considerable. The *moral* of the Allied troops was excellent.

This statement was supplemented by a statement issued from the French Embassy:—

To the west of the Meuse the British Army, which was on our left, was attacked by the Germans. Admirable under fire, it resisted the enemy with its usual coolness.

The French Army which was operating in this region advanced

BRITISH LIGHT CAVALRY charging GERMAN CUIRASSIERS

to the attack. Two army corps, which were in the first line, spurred on by their dash, were received by a very murderous fire. They did not give way, but, being subjected to a counter-attack by the Prussian Guard, they ultimately had to fall back. They did not do so until they had inflicted enormous losses on their adversaries.

On the east of the Meuse our troops marched forward through a very difficult country. Vigorously attacked on the outskirts of the forest, they had to fall back after a very lively fight to the south of the Semoy River.

On the orders of General Joffre our troops and the British troops took up positions on the covering line, which they would not have left had not the admirable Belgian effort enabled them to enter Belgium. They are intact.

Our cavalry has not suffered at all. Our artillery has affirmed its superiority. Our officers and our soldiers are in the best physical and moral state.

In consequence of the orders given the fighting will change its aspect for some days. The French will remain for a time on the defensive. At the proper time chosen by headquarters it will resume a vigorous offensive.

Our losses are considerable. It would be premature to enumerate them. The same holds good for those of the German army, which has nevertheless suffered so much as to be obliged to arrest its counter-attack movement in order to take up fresh positions.

Although some vigorous fighting had been going on during Sunday morning, August 23, the extreme peril of our troops was not realised until late in the afternoon, when Sir John French received tidings of extreme gravity that large reinforcements of the enemy were advancing towards the British lines. This enormous host of Germans, strengthened no doubt with troops released from Namur, was hurling itself forward furiously, and the British left wing on the west was especially threatened with a dangerous flanking movement from the enemy. On the east towards Charleroi the position was equally perilous, because no support could be expected in that direction, as the French troops had already withdrawn. Sir John French therefore ordered a retirement, which began on Sunday evening and continued till the following morning.

GERMAN INFANTRY FIRING FROM TRENCHES

But the men fell back unwillingly, while they engaged in a terrific conflict with the oncoming forces of the enemy. Everything possible was done by the Germans to harass the British and to convert their withdrawal into a rout. With the aid of powerful searchlights, which continuously swept towards the country selected for the retirement of our troops, the enemy endeavoured to deprive them of the advantage of the night, and covered them with a murderous hail of shot and shell. But, as we know, the plans of the Germans failed owing to the skill of our generals and to the splendid nerve of our men: our lines remained intact and their spirit unbroken.

Mr. Alfred J. Rorke, special correspondent of the Central News, sent the following early account of the fighting at Mons:—

Paris, Monday (received per Courier, Tuesday). Graphic stories of how the British troops at Mons fought during the two days in which they bore the brunt of the main German advance reached Paris in the early hours of this morning, when officers arriving from the front reported at the War Office, and, in subsequent conversation with their closest personal friends, told of the wonderful coolness and daring of our men. The shooting of our infantry on the firing line, they said, was wonderful. Every time a German's head showed above the trenches and every time the German infantry attempted to rush a position there came a withering rifle fire from the khaki-clad forms lying in extended formation along a big battle front.

The firing was not the usual firing of nervous men, shooting without aiming and sometimes without rhyme or reason, as is so often the case in warfare. It was rather the calm, calculated riflemanship of the men one sees on the Stickledown range firing with all the artificial aids permitted to the match rifle expert whose one concern is prize money.

When quick action was necessary the firing and the action of the men was only that of prize riflemen firing at a disappearing target. There was no excitement, no nervousness; just cool, methodical efficiency. If the British lost heavily heaven only knows what the Germans must have lost, because, as one of their wounded officers (whom the British took prisoner) remarked, "We had never expected anything like it; it was staggering."

The British troops went to their positions silently but happily.

There was no singing, because that was forbidden, but as the khaki-clad columns deployed and began to crawl to the trenches there were various sallies of humour in the different dialects of English, Irish, and Scottish counties. The Yorkshireman, for instance, would draw a comparison between the men they were going to fight and certain dogs that won't fight which the Yorkshire collier has not time to waste upon at the pit-head; the Cockney soldier was there with his sallies about "Uncle Bill," and every Irishman who went into the firing line wished he had the money to buy a little Irish horse, so that he could have a slap at the *Uhlans*.

And the cavalry! Officers coming from the front declare that our cavalrymen charged the much-vaunted German horsemen as Berserkers might have done. When they got into action with tunics open, and sometimes without tunics at all, they flung themselves at the German horsemen in a manner which surprised even their own officers, who had themselves expected great things of them. The *Uhlans*, whose name and fearful fame had spread terror among the Belgian peasants and the frontier villages of France, were just the sort of men the British troopers were waiting for. The Britishers, mostly Londoners, who, as Wellington said, make the best cavalry soldiers in the world, were dying to have a cut at them; and when they got into clinches the *Uhlans* had the surprise of their lives.

From the scene of battle, the point of interest in the European war drama, as far as England is concerned, shifted in the small hours of this morning to the railway station at X, where officers and men of the Army Service Corps awaited the arrival of the wounded—the British wounded from the firing line. Everything was perfectly organised; there was no theatrical display; the officers and men of the British Army waited silently and calmly for the toll of war, which they had been advised was on its way.

The West Kents were one of the first of the British troops to come under fire at Mons, in which they lost four officers killed, including Major Pach-Beresford, and four officers and seventeen men wounded, A wounded lance-corporal of this regiment says:—

We reached Mons on Saturday afternoon, August 22, the day before the battle. We at once commenced to entrench, and were still engaged on this work when the Germans fired their first

9TH LANCERS

shell, which wrecked a house about twenty yards away. Then we got ready for the fight. We made loopholes in a wall near the house, and remained there for fifteen hours under a heavy fire of shrapnel. The Germans came across the valley in front of us in thousands, but their rifle fire was absolutely rotten, and such damage as they did was caused by the big guns which covered their advance. Numerically the Germans were far superior to us, and as soon as one lot was shot down another took its place.

We retired from Mons about four o'clock on Monday morning to a little village on the borders of France. We kept up a rearguard action all the way, and it was in this that I was wounded. A shell dropped close to me, and some fragments penetrated my left leg. I was thrown to the ground, and for a time lay unconscious. When I recovered I found my rifle and ammunition were missing, having, I suppose, been taken by the Germans, who evidently thought I was dead.

The lance-corporal eventually managed to reach St. Quentin.

A private of the same regiment told a thrilling story of the battle:—

It was Sunday, August 23 that we were at Mons, billeted in a farmyard, and we were having a sing-song and watching people home from church. The Belgian ladies were very kind-hearted, and we were given their prayer-books as souvenirs, and they also went to the shops and bought us cigarettes, which were most acceptable to the troops. At about 12.30 an orderly had gone down to draw dinners, when an aeroplane appeared overhead, throwing out some black powder. After this shrapnel burst overhead, acquainting us of the fact that the Germans were in the vicinity.

All was confusion and uproar for the moment, because we were not armed, and our shirts and socks were out to wash, that being the only chance we had to get them washed. It did not take us long, however, to get in fighting trim and to go through the town to the scene of operations, which was on the other side of a small canal that adjoined Mons. Here we found the A Company of the Royal West Kents engaged in a hard tussle in keeping off the enemy until support arrived. The A Company had been engaged in outpost duty, so that they were the first to

A MOUNTED UHLAN

meet the enemy. Their casualties were very heavy, and they lost all of their officers except Lieut. Bell, who showed great valour in going out to bring in the wounded. Most of the damage was done by the shells, although at times the enemy were within 300 yards of our troops. We arrived in the nick of time,, and took up position in a glass-blowing factory. We loop-holed the walls and held that position until darkness set in. With darkness upon us we fixed bayonets, and lay in wait in case the enemy made an attempt to rush us.

About eleven p.m. we received orders to retire over the canal. Two sections of C Company were left to keep the enemy in check, whilst the remainder of the battalion retired. After all had crossed the bridge was blown up, so that we were likely to be left in peace until the Germans could find a means of crossing the river. The two sections of C Company that had been left behind, unfortunately, were unable to retire over the bridge before it was blown up, and they had to find their own ways and means of getting across. Most of them managed to do so. We retired from the town of Mons, and got into open country, but we still kept on moving throughout the night.

When daylight arrived we saw that Mons had been practically demolished, and that the Germans were also firing at times at the hospital. Throughout the morning we continued to fight a rearguard action. We did not leave off trekking until six in the evening, when we found ourselves well out of the range of the German artillery in a valley surrounded by large hills. Here all the troops were glad to lie down and get something to eat, as we had been without food since the previous morning.

Hungry soldiers were thankful to go into the swede and turnip fields and make a meal of these roots as though they were apples. We found the French and Belgian people very kind to us on the line of march. They would stand at the wayside and give us fruit, and they had large tubs of water ready, and this the troops very much appreciated.

About eight o'clock all lights were ordered to be put out and no noise to be made, and we all lay down for a well-earned rest after two trying days, putting out pickets in case of surprise. About an hour before dawn we were all ordered to stand to arms, and the column was once more engaged in a retiring movement.

As the column was on the march, I saw a duel in the air between French and German aeroplanes. It was wonderful to see the Frenchman manoeuvre to get the upper position of the German, and after about ten minutes or a quarter of an hour the Frenchman got on top, and blazed away with a revolver on the German. He injured him so much as to cause him to descend, and when found he was dead. The British troops buried the airman and burnt the aeroplane.

During that day we were not troubled by any more German aeroplanes, and about five p.m. a halt was ordered, and we took things comfortably, hoping to have a rest until daylight came again. We were fortunate enough not to be disturbed that night, and at dawn we again stood to arms, and we found the Germans close upon our heels. The column got on the move, and several regiments were ordered to entrench themselves. We found it very hot and fatiguing work with such small tools to use. We soon found, however, that "*where there's a will there's a way*," and quickly entrenched ourselves so as to be protected from the artillery fire.

It was not long before the German artillery found our trenches and gave us rather a warm time. Our own artillery had to open fire at 2,100 yards, which was very close for artillery. I saw a battery in front of us put out of action. There were only about six men left amongst them, and they were engaged in trying to get away the guns. This disaster was due to the accurate shell firing of the German artillery.

In their efforts the brave gunners were not successful, owing to their horses being killed. It was interesting to see an officer engaged in walking round the guns and putting them out of action, or in other words seeing that they would be of no use to the Germans. This action required a great deal of bravery under the circumstances, because the enemy continued to keep up the heavy firing. Much bravery was also displayed by wounded comrades of the battery helping one another to get out of the firing line.

About this time the enemy were advancing, owing to the superiority of numbers, and hand-to-hand fighting had taken place in the right trenches. Owing to the artillery firing being so heavy, and the British being in such comparatively small numbers, the officer in charge of my company deemed it wise

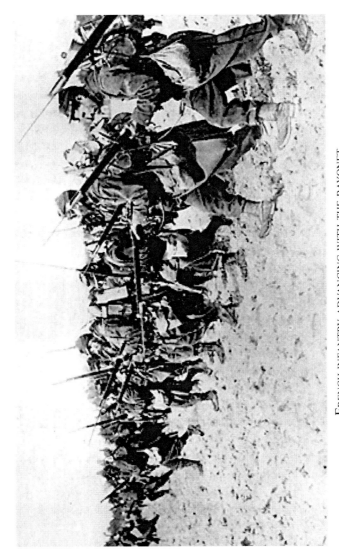

FRENCH INFANTRY ADVANCING WITH THE BAYONET

to retire. It was rather late, however, and he said to the men who were in the trenches: "Now, boys, every man for himself." Having got these orders, we were not long in doing a retiring movement and trying to save our own skins. It was hard to see my own comrades being cut down like corn owing to the deadly shrapnel firing.

I was wounded at this point by a bullet from a maxim gun. I staggered at the time, thinking my hand had been blown off; but I recovered and kept on the run, and got in a trench, where I bandaged myself up. From there I continued to retire on my own, as I had lost touch with my section. I ran into the general commanding, and he asked me what was the matter with me. I told him I was wounded, and he said, "For God's sake, man, don't go into the hospital; they are blowing it up now." I did not want telling that twice, and I started to track down country to get into touch with the column, where I knew the ambulance men were, and they would dress my wound.

When I got to the ambulance wagons I found they were mostly full with wounded who were in a far worse plight than I was. So I went along with the column, and a motor lorry came by and I got a lift to St. Quentin.

A wounded corporal of the Royal Engineers said:

So awful was the fighting that it is wonderful that anybody ever came out of it alive. I have no idea how we did come through,

The corporal and his comrades were ordered to build a pontoon bridge over the Mons Canal. This work was begun early on the Sunday morning, August 23, in the face of a murderous rifle and shell fire. Gradually the bridge was pushed over, until it was almost within touch of the bank held by the enemy. Man after man of the British Engineers was hit, but still the rest stuck to their task, heedless of the rain of missiles all around.

Late in the afternoon the corporal was standing in the water assisting in the construction, when a shrapnel shell wounded him in the right arm. He made for the bank, only to find that his boots, which he had removed, had disappeared. He bound up his wounded arm with his handkerchief, and soon afterwards work on the bridge was abandoned.

Orders were given to get to cover the best way possible, and to wait until darkness fell. Then our troops fell back owing to the overwhelming numbers of the Germans. The corporal removed his *putties*, bound them round his feet, and started to retire. In the darkness, however, he lost the main body of the British, and wandered away to the west.

After a while he met a wounded Gordon Highlander, who had had his teeth shot away, and was also lost. The Highlander bound up the engineer's arm with his first field dressing, and the two men snatched what sleep they could under a hedge. Their breakfast next morning was a raw swede, pulled up from one of the fields.

Throughout that day they trudged on and on through a deserted country, but as night fell they came to some cottages scattered on the roadside. The inhabitants, recognising them as British, welcomed the wanderers, and gave them a good meal of bread and butter, cheese, and rabbit. They also allowed the soldiers to sleep there that night, and early in the morning directed them to Boussu, a town some miles further on in the direction of Lille.

Creeping slowly and painfully along, under cover of the hedges as far as possible, the men saw large parties of *Uhlans* scouting a short distance ahead. Fortunately a small wood was near by, and, turning into it, they lay concealed under some bushes for nearly eight hours. Several times the enemy approached within fifty yards of the fugitives, who almost feared to breathe. At length, towards evening, the coast became clear, and the two men were able to continue their journey.

After another night in the open air Boussu was reached on the following morning. From there they were sent on to Lille, and afterwards to Le Havre and England.

Sergeant Bird and Private Woolgar, of the 4th Dragoon Guards, also had the misfortune to miss their regiment. They said:—

It was when we were sent out under General Allenby to help the left wing, which was hard pressed, that our misfortunes began. Our horses were shot under us, but we struggled after our men as best we could until we picked up some German horses, all of which bore the mark K 4 on the reins. We had hardly got going again when we had these shot under us by the German artillery, with the result that we were stranded absolutely on our own, and you can guess our feelings as we saw our squadron moving away on the right. We were all more or less injured. One of our chaps had his arms split right open, and calmly said, "I say, boys, do you think I'm hurt?"

We endeavoured to get the wounded to a neighbouring farm-

BRITISH CAVALRYMAN TAKING RATIONS

house, and succeeded in taking several there, but on going back with the last batch were refused admission, as by this time the occupants could see the Germans bearing down in that direction in force. We then made for the fowl-house and hid there, but our position was very dangerous, as it was not long before the Germans began to enter in order to wash their wounds at the little well in the corner.

Sergeant Bird continued:

It was pitch dark at the time, and I found the most comfortable position for me was sitting in a basket, which, I realised after a few moments and by certain signs, had contained a dozen eggs in the straw. The artillery were now in action, and the British seemed to have found the spot, as the tiles of our hiding-place began to fall in, and we found it advisable to put baskets over our heads as well; otherwise they would have been split open by the flying tiles and fragments of shells.

When night came we decided to endeavour to escape from our perilous position, and just outside the door we found a German sentry, who seemed to be scouting for British fugitives. We passed quite close to him, but didn't stop to say "Goodnight." How we did it I can't for the life of me tell you, but we did it, and then made off as we thought towards the British lines, but to our disgust found we were going right into the German lines. We decided, therefore, to anchor there for the night and get away in the morning. We found this was the German Headquarters Staff, so that we can say we dined with the German generals that night, the only difference being that they were inside and we were outside; they were having wines, &c., and we had swedes and no &c.

In the morning we had to dodge sentries, but found that presented little difficulty. We decided then to travel south-west, with the sun as our guide. To do this, however, was impossible, for in our wanderings we had day after day to dodge German troops, who were continually marching across our tracks. We can hardly describe what happened during this time, but the harrowing sights we saw will never be effaced from our memories. Our condition was terrible, for we were at one time reduced to five biscuits between three of us, and these had to suffice us for three days. Sometimes we were afraid to drink water because we heard it was poisoned. At last we met the British.

Private Alexander Andrews, of the Royal Scots, spoke of the deadly havoc of the shrapnel:—

> But the German infantry could not hit the place they belong to. We could not help hitting them. We saw them first about 800 yards away, and they came along in bunches just like a crowd leaving a football match. Our Maxims simply struck them down, and I will guarantee that for every one that fell on our side they lost ten or twelve. It was "rapid firing," and we gave it them hot. None in our trench was killed, and we had only five or six, including myself, injured with shrapnel. A piece of shrapnel struck me on the top of the left ankle about half-past seven o'clock, cutting through my boot and making me feel a little queer. I bandaged it up, and went off with the others when the order came to retire about one o'clock on the Monday morning.
>
> Mons was in flames by that time, and the German big guns had been blazing about all night. We had been in a tight corner— two regiments against thousands, as most of us believe—and I would like to say a word for our captain, Captain Hill Whitson. In the trenches on the Sunday night, August 23, he was walking about with his revolver, ready for anything, and cheering us up while the shrapnel played about our position. Well, as I said, we had to retire. We went back three or four miles. The first regiment we saw was the Gordons, and I took particular notice that they had a German prisoner in the front of their ranks.

The aeroplanes were employed with great skill by the Germans, before opening fire, to take observations for the range of their artillery, and the precise locality of our soldiers. It was, moreover, evident that they possessed an intimate knowledge of the country where the fighting took place. Owing to the enormous number of the German reserves, when one regiment was vanquished another was always ready to take its place, and so they advanced like an avalanche.

The slaughter was awful: the British suffered terribly, but the German losses were appalling. It is stated that in some places the dead of the enemy was piled up to a height of six feet, and that to pass over them the Germans made bridges of the corpses of their own men.

Here, as elsewhere,, the Germans resorted to cowardly brutality. Their cavalry are said to have driven women and children in front

BRITISH CAVALRY RETURNING FROM MONS

of them in the streets, to protect them from the British fire. But the enemy lost as well as gained reputations: Sir Philip Chetwode, the cavalry leader, after fighting without ceasing for ten days, with odds of five to one against them, said, "We have been through the *Uhlans* like brown paper."

Innumerable cases of personal heroism have been recalled. That of Captain Grenfell must not be omitted. Although suffering from two severe wounds, he participated in the rescue of two British guns, after shrapnel shell had burst over them and struck the artillerymen who were serving them. This act enabled troopers of the 9th Lancers under his direction to get away.

According to the statement of the Paris correspondent of the *Daily Telegraph,* gathered from the reports of Belgian and British fugitives, between Saturday and Monday, August 22-24, the British Expeditionary Force bore the brunt of six furious attacks made by six distinct German columns, which were all repulsed successfully, though with considerable loss. The Allies raised a veritable hecatomb of German corpses near Mons. At different points on the battlefield, the bodies of Germans were heaped up so that in the course of their furious charge the Turcos experienced great difficulty in coming into contact with the enemy.

We can picture our men fighting doggedly on, in the din and carnage of the engagement, during those hot August days and calm clear nights, with the never-ceasing crack of rifle-shots, the boom of the artillery fire and the scream of the shells, while the enemy came on with relentless and unending regularity.

CHAPTER 3

The Fall of Namur

Shifting the scene for a time to the operations on the French lines, we obtain a view of the fighting in the neighbourhood of Charleroi on the eve of the great battle on the Belgian frontier, from the description of a correspondent to a Paris paper, and communicated by Mr. A. Beaumont:—

Our troops in conformity with the plan laid down for them are harassing the Germans on the right and the left banks of the Meuse, keeping in constant contact with them, killing as many of their scouting parties as possible.

I witnessed on Friday morning, August 21, a series of engagements of this kind outside the suburbs of Charleroi. I saw our outposts everywhere, and heard rifle-fire here and there, with now and then troopers coming in and bringing prisoners with them.

Our cavalry was in splendid form, and eager for action. Two hundred yards from a certain bridge I saw seven *Uhlans* coming out of a wood. Three of them were shot down at once, and the remainder hurriedly fled.

On my return to Charleroi I learn that a detachment of twenty Hussars of the Death's Head, led by an officer, had entered the upper town at seven in the morning. They proceeded towards the Sambre, and quietly said, "Good morning" to the people at the doors. "*Bon jour, bon jour,*" they said to the housewives, who were looking on in wonder, and who, mistaking their khaki uniform, took them for English soldiers.

People even enthusiastically raised cheers for England. The soldiers, also misled, allowed them to pass. An officer finally saw

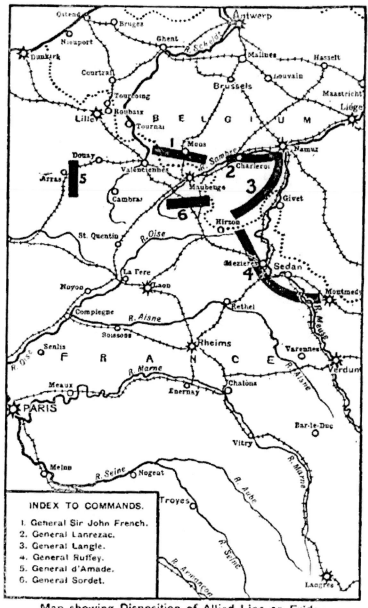

INDEX TO COMMANDS.

1. General Sir John French.
2. General Lanrezac.
3. General Langle.
4. General Ruffey.
5. General d'Amade.
6. General Sordet.

Map showing Disposition of Allied Line on Friday,
August 21.

them from a window, and rushed down to a detachment on guard in the Rue Pont Neuf, and gave the alarm. A number of infantry soldiers at once opened fire on them. It was at the corner of the Rue de Montigny, where the tramway and railway lines pass.

Three of the intruders were shot down, and the rest, with their officer, took to flight. It was not believed that such a thing would be possible, but it proved that the Germans are capable of anything. They did the same thing many a time in 1870.

At two in the afternoon the guns were heard in the north. The Germans, coming from Eghezee, had placed heavy batteries and siege guns in position before Namur. But the Namur forts immediately sent such a murderous and accurate fire in reply that, in less than half an hour, the German battery was silenced, and half the guns demolished.

Another line of attack chosen by the Germans was between Brand L'Alleud and Genappe, over a front of some ten to twelve miles. The German batteries here met with the same fate.

A day later the same writer said, in writing from Jeumont:—

I left Charleroi last night for Jeumont, on the French frontier, but not a bit too soon. It was high time. This very morning the engineers of the Northern railway line witnessed the attack on Charleroi.

The Germans, from the outskirts of the upper town, were sending shells on the railway station and on salient parts of the lower town. They were trying to force a passage across the bridges over the Sambre. Fugitives from all sides arrive here (at Jeumont) by the last trains. After two o'clock in the afternoon the guns were distinctly heard, first from the direction of Charleroi, then from Thuin.

The Germans are being met by the English. This is the beginning of the great battle which has been expected.

An account of the French operations on Saturday, August 22, was printed in *La Liberté* from the description of a railway official on the Belgian frontier. The official said:—

It was on Saturday, towards nightfall, that we heard the first sound of the cannon. We had known, however, for several hours that strong German forces were preparing to attack the allied

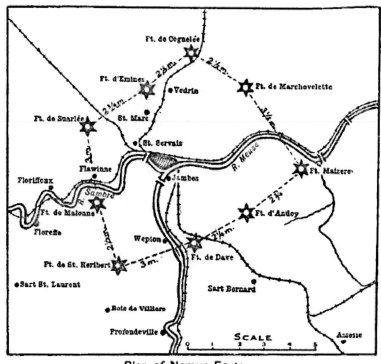

Plan of Namur Forts.

armies massed on the banks of the Sambre, and that a great battle was imminent. All night long, without cessation, the cannonading continued. Till dawn we had no news of the battle. On Sunday morning we learned from wounded soldiers on their way to Maubeuge that the battle was engaged all along the line, and shortly afterwards we heard the sound of heavy firing to the north. From noon onwards we could distinctly see the flight of shrapnel through the air, and from the top of the motor-house, situated on rising ground, could follow the phases of the artillery duel.

We soon saw that the Germans' fire was badly directed. They rarely hit their mark. On the other hand, the English artillery fire, which held the heights round Mons, was admirable in its precision, and wrought terrible loss among the massed German troops. We remained all Sunday night on our observatory, and at dawn we had the conviction that the English very definitely had the upper hand, and that the German attack had been repulsed.

However, the news which reached us during the evening from environs of Charleroi was anything but good. It was said that the town had been taken and retaken several times, and had been subjected to a terrible bombardment, which had reduced it practically to ruins. At two o'clock on Monday morning a cyclist messenger informed us that the French had once more occupied the town. He said that the Germans before leaving it had set it on fire, and that the French troops would find it difficult to maintain their position there. In any case, the cannonade became louder during the night, and at daybreak shells were bursting within a quarter of a mile of the station.

Later in the morning of Monday we received orders to evacuate the station, which was now becoming untenable. We were told that, the French having been outnumbered on the east of Charleroi, the allied troops had been compelled to retire on the frontier. When we were leaving the station and getting into the carriage, we heard the sound of joyous shouts from the road. We went out to see what had happened, and to our stupefaction saw a detachment of seven *Uhlans* commanded by an officer. The inhabitants, unfamiliar with foreign uniforms, had taken them for English cavalry. The error was soon discovered. A French captain on service in the station shot the German of-

ROYAL ARTILLERY

ficer through the head, and a patrol of mounted *chasseurs* rode up and took the men prisoners.

The defence of Charleroi by the French against the overwhelming hosts of the Germans was a marvel of audacity and courage.

Two inhabitants of Auvelais, a straggling village with a population of about 8,000, situated between Charleroi and Namur, gave the following account of what they have witnessed:—
'Our village occupies both banks of the Sambre, the portion on the left bank being divided into two by the main road leading from Genappe to Eghezee. Since Sunday week German aeroplanes have been flying over the country, and one was pursued, though unsuccessfully, by a French machine. Many French troops passed and were received with enthusiasm. On Thursday evening, August 20, a patrol of *Uhlans* suddenly appeared on the road. The French horsemen were in their saddles at once, and left the village at full gallop, their swords flashing in the air. They overtook the *Uhlans* at Balatre, and attacked them, killing six and returning without any loss to themselves.

At eight o'clock next morning firing began. The Germans advanced by the main road, literally crawling along the ground, and stopping now and then to fire. Just at this time a German aeroplane dropped a bomb on a factory, but without doing any damage. By ten o'clock the firing on both sides was terrific. From where we were we saw six French soldiers fall. Suddenly the French artillery came into action, and until midday the guns fired continuously with terrible effect. On the other hand, a German shell, which struck the roof of a house opposite us, rolled into the road without exploding, and we saw many others which also failed to explode. The Germans took shelter in the houses on the left bank, and the French infantry were ordered to retire in order that the artillery might dislodge the enemy.

In five minutes everything was burning. Other Germans came through the woods and entered the town, where they behaved like madmen. They smashed in doors with their rifle butts and threw special burning cartridges into the houses. We were warned that it was time for us to escape, but we saw some terrible scenes. A woman who had forgotten to bring some clothing for her baby, and who returned to obtain it, was seized by the

Germans. They made her march before them, and at the end of about 200 yards killed her. The French, though inferior in numbers, resisted splendidly, and the Germans were compelled to halt.

The artillery duel was then resumed. Everything round our house was burning furiously, and we had to abandon all. When we arrived at Esau the soldiers made us crawl along the edge of a wood. The bullets were whistling above us, and of the forty people in our party only three dared to pass. At Chatelet we met strong bodies of French troops, and at eight in the evening we left for Charleroi.

The fighting, however, had spread, and we had to go further. At 8.30 the last train left. A German aeroplane dropped a bomb within twenty yards of us, and though all the glass in the station was broken, no one was hurt. We thought we might reach Mons, but there was fighting there, and we were taken to the frontier and thence to Paris.'

A criticism came from a wounded gunner. "If we lose many men," he said, "it is the fault of the infantry. They go ahead too quickly, and end by interfering with our fire."

A French Zouave officer, who returned wounded from the front, related the following. His regiment took part in the fighting round Charleroi when the Prussian Guard Regiments suffered so severely.

Describing the effect of the German artillery, the officer said that the shells when they burst produce a series of terrific explosions, but do comparatively little damage. The soldiers quickly perceiving their chief characteristic is noise soon get accustomed to them. One man who was struck in the back by a splinter of shell was merely bruised.

On the other hand the French artillery fire had a deadly effect. Its accuracy was little short of marvellous. For instance, he saw a German battery appearing in the distance, and even before it could unlimber it was destroyed by the French fire.

The ravages caused by the French artillery were enormous. Whole ranks of infantry were mown down by the shrapnel, some of those shot dead remaining standing owing to the numbers of bodies accumulated round them.

The officer estimated the German casualties during three days of fighting at between 50,000 and 60,000, far exceeding the French losses. He confirmed acts of untold cruelty perpetrated by the Germans.

A COLUMN OF FRENCH CAVALRY

The French soldiers were enraged by their practice of finishing off the wounded. One officer, severely wounded while his regiment was retreating, was so convinced of the fate in store for him that he blew his brains out.

The Germans seemed to delight in wanton destruction. At nightfall their lines were lit up by burning villages on the horizon.

When asked his opinion regarding the military value of the German troops, the officer said that their bravery was wonderful, especially that of the Imperial Guard, which did not flinch before a most murderous fire.

On the other hand, the *moral* of the French troops was splendid. They were not in the least disheartened by a temporary check, and were convinced that if well led they would achieve wonders.

A number of French soldiers wounded in the battle of Charleroi reached Chartres soon after the battle. A soldier in the Colonial Infantry gave his impressions of his part of the fierce fighting—naturally a restricted part:

> I only saw a tiny morsel of the battle. With our African comrades we advanced against the Prussian Guard. The bullets sang continuously above our heads. We advanced by short rushes, taking advantage of the smallest cover. We were as if intoxicated by the wine of battle. I do not know how long our advance lasted. All I remember is that our last shots were fired at fifty yards distance from the enemy. Then we rushed forward and attacked them with cold steel. Had we been more fortunate our attack would have given us the victory.
>
> There are no troops in the world, however courageous they may be, who can stand against a bayonet attack of our African soldiers. Unhappily, our charge was broken by a withering fire from machine guns which the Germans had concealed in the ruins of an old factory. We had to retire with severe loss, but it is consoling to think that the Prussian Guard must have suffered at least as heavily.

Several wounded soldiers of an infantry regiment also gave their impressions on that part of the Titanic struggle in which they were engaged. They said that the Prussian marksmanship was not good. They fired too low. Besides, when the French advanced in skirmishing line, they protected their breast with their packs. These improvised bucklers deadened the force of the enemy's bullets. The German practice with the machine-guns, on the other hand, was deadly, but the position of these guns was easily discovered, and when discovered they were speedily silenced by the French seventy-fives. The Turcos, who, though the most formidable of fighters, have an ineradicable strain of childishness in their nature, seem to have supplied very helpful comic relief.

One of them captured a German officer, carefully disarmed him, and was leading him off to the rear, when the officer began cursing him in broken French. Our Turco's first impulse was to kill his prisoner, but he thought better and more wisely of it. He decided to humiliate him. Accordingly, at the bayonet-point, he compelled the officer to carry his pack, and, to put the finishing touch to the humiliation, placed his regimental *gamelle*, or saucepan, on the prisoner's head. The entry of the Turco into camp, preceded by a Prussian major, crowned with a saucepan and performing an *impromptu* goose-step at the point of the bayonet, was highly successful.

While the British troops were fighting at Mons and the French were engaged at Charleroi, Namur was in the last throes of siege. The strategic value of its position at the confluence of the rivers Sambre and Meuse rendered it of supreme importance to the Allies, and the fame of its forts was such as to raise high expectations as to their powers of endurance. The unexpected news, therefore, of the fall of Namur on August 23 was received with dismay, because it was believed that after the siege of Liège it could make a stout resistance with the support of the Allied armies. But for several days the fortress had been practically isolated as the French were not sufficiently advanced to render it much aid, and its fall was due to the tremendous fire of the German siege guns.

Some of these howitzers were stated to have been 11 inches (28 cm.) calibre, and to have required teams of 35 horses to move them. Of these guns there were some thirty batteries in action, with one or two guns to a battery. A number of howitzers concentrated simultaneously on each fort and smothered it with fire. The Germans are said to have attacked in a formation three ranks deep, the front rank lying down, the second kneeling, and the third standing. They afforded a target, which was fully used, for machine-gun fire. The Turcos fought well against the German Guard Corps, but while attacking they were trapped by Germans sounding their charge at 600 yards, and they were "badly mauled" at 300 yards from the German position.

M. Auguste Mellot, the deputy of the town said:

The inhabitants of Namur had hopes until Thursday, August 13, that the Belgian Army, joined by the French and English, would meet the forces of General von Emmich and rout them before they reached Namur. But on that day the Belgian horsemen met a detachment of Uhlans who were much more numerous than usual. Although they were repulsed, not without a hard struggle, by the Belgian lancers and *carbineers*, they did not doubt that the Germans would return in greater force. Preparations were therefore made in Namur for a strong resistance. But while they were thus occupied, the first three shells burst over the town on August 14. One of them struck the bridge of Salzinnes in the midst of a gathering of onlookers, five of whom were killed. From that moment they received shells every day. There were more killed in consequence, not to speak of the material damage done. On Saturday, August 15, the cannonade was distinctly heard at Dinant, where the Germans were trying to force the passage over the Meuse, and were repulsed by the fire from the French machine guns. After this it was thought that the Allied armies would be able to drive the Germans out of Belgium. However, the German cavalry came nearer and nearer to Namur every day. Information was then received that the railway line was cut. The mail from Brussels failed to arrive regularly.

On August 18 the anxiety of the inhabitants increased. The German cavalry had been seen at a place in the neighbourhood and it was evident that they were being surrounded. On Thursday, August 20, their fears became still greater. They gave up hopes of hearing of a decisive battle north of Namur. News had arrived of the occupation of Brussels, and no one was permitted to pass between the lines of the forts, even with a permit.

During the night the cannonade began all around Namur. On August 21 the battle around the town became general and lasted all day. While eleven German Army Corps were passing the Meuse, coming from Bisé, a powerful force was detailed to mask their march, and kept up a heavy fire on our positions. The German attacks were multiplied the whole time, and their fire extended over a line of some ten miles on the left bank of the Meuse, and over a similar line of the right bank of the same river. During that time the French forces sent to meet them tried to check the German advance.

By five p.m. on August 23 Namur was completely evacuated,

BELGIAN INFANTRY

the defenders finding themselves unable to support the heavy artillery fire.

A Belgian soldier, who pays a high tribute to the courage of our men, in a letter to a relative in England says:—

Many of us have been able to see for ourselves the wonderful phlegm of the British soldiers. They are born warriors. They are soldiers by predilection as much as by trade. Most of them have taken part in numerous campaigns, and many fought in the Boer War, in which they gained precious experience. We have listened with admiration to the glorious accounts which our chivalrous French neighbours have given to the world of the British soldiers' coolness and tenacity in the fight near the village of Quaregnon, where twenty-six Britishers routed more than 3,500 Germans. The fight was witnessed by some of our own staff, and the story is absolutely authentic.

It happened after the different battles which resulted in the evacuation of Mons. The Britishers, who had fought like heroes, must have retreated with reluctance in obedience, it is true, to orders received from the military authorities. As they were only giving ground step by step twenty-six fusiliers entrenched themselves in a farm overlooking the long, straight road leading to Quaregnon. They were in possession of several *mitrailleuses*, and they made holes in the farm door, three lines of three holes in superposition, and placed their *mitrailleuses* in position.

"Now, boys," shouted one of the twenty-six, "we are going to cinematograph the grey devils when they come along. This is going to be Coronation Day. Let each of us take as many pictures as possible."

As soon as the Germans appeared on the road and started attacking the canal bridge the fusiliers very coolly turned the handle of their deadly guns, commencing with the lower tier, and with the same placidity as a bioscope operator would have done.

The picture witnessed from the farm on the "living screen" by the canal bridge was one that will not easily be forgotten. The "grey devils," as the Germans are now commonly called, dropped down in hundreds like those tin soldiers (made in Germany) which our children arrange in long lines on the table and which fall in one big mass when the first one is slightly touched with the finger. In a few minutes the corpses were heaping up. Then followed another onslaught by the *mitrailleuses* placed against the upper part of the door, followed immediately by a fresh deadly sweep and by another one.

The Germans, however, found out their difficult position, which exposed them to this destructive fire, and they resolutely took a turning move, and made straight for the farm. When they got there they found neither guns nor fusiliers, but only an opening in a party wall, through which the plucky operators had disappeared with their apparatus.

There was nothing left for the Germans but to continue their march along the road, which gets narrower just before entering the village. They had not gone more than 200 yards before a fresh rain of lead, which was kept going for a long time, and mowed them down like grass, and in still more considerable numbers than at the first fight. With a wild rush the remainder of the Germans, about 150, stormed the door of the new farm which sheltered the enemy, but found only the *mitrailleuses*, conscientiously put out of order. As for the twenty-six heroes, they had disappeared like a conjurer's rabbit, to rejoin their regiment, without having sustained the slightest injury, after having routed 3,500 Germans.

CHAPTER 4

Sir John French's Account of the Events of August 25

We now return to Sir John French's despatch and quote that portion in which he describes the causes that forced him to retire to the Bavai—Maubeuge line on Monday, August 24:—

> In view of the possibility of my being driven from the Mons position, I had previously ordered a position in rear to be reconnoitred. This position rested on the fortress of Maubeuge on the right and extended west to Jenlain, south-east of Valenciennes, on the left. The position was reported difficult to hold, because standing crops and buildings made the sighting of trenches very difficult and limited the field of fire in many important localities. It nevertheless afforded a few good artillery positions.
>
> When the news of the retirement of the French and the heavy German threatening on my front reached me, I endeavoured to confirm it by aeroplane reconnaissance; and as a result of this I determined to effect a retirement to the Maubeuge position at daybreak on the 24th.
>
> A certain amount of fighting continued along the whole line throughout the night, and at daybreak on the 24th the 2nd Division from the neighbourhood of Harmignies made a powerful demonstration as if to retake Binche. This was supported by the artillery of both the 1st and 2nd Divisions, whilst the 1st Division took up a supporting position in the neighbourhood of Peissant. Under cover of this demonstration the Second Corps retired on the line Dour—Quarouble—Frameries. The

3rd Division on the right of the Corps suffered considerable loss in this operation from the enemy, who had retaken Mons.

The Second Corps halted on this line, where they partially entrenched themselves, enabling Sir Douglas Haig with the First Corps gradually to withdraw to the new position; and he effected this without much further loss, reaching the line Bavai—Maubeuge about 7 p.m. Towards midday the enemy appeared to be directing his principal effort against our left.

I had previously ordered General Allenby with the cavalry to act vigorously in advance of my left front and endeavour to take the pressure off.

About 7.30 a.m. General Allenby received a message from Sir George Fergusson, commanding 5th Division, saying that he was very hard pressed and in urgent need of support. On receipt of this message General Allenby drew in the cavalry and endeavoured to bring direct support to the 5th Division.

During the course of this operation General De Lisle, of the 2nd Cavalry Brigade, thought he saw a good opportunity to paralyse the further advance of the enemy's infantry by making a mounted attack on his flank. He formed up and advanced for this purpose, but was held up by wire about 500 yards from his objective, and the 9th Lancers and 18th Hussars suffered severely in the retirement of the brigade.

The 19th Infantry Brigade, which had been guarding the Line of Communications, was brought up by rail to Valenciennes on the 22nd and 23rd. On the morning of the 24th they were moved out to a position south of Quarouble to support the left flank of the Second Corps.

With the assistance of the cavalry Sir Horace Smith-Dorrien was enabled to effect his retreat to a new position; although, having two corps of the enemy on his front and one threatening his flank, he suffered great losses m doing so.

At nightfall the position was occupied by the Second Corps to the west of Bavai, the First Corps to the right. The right was protected by the Fortress of Maubeuge, the left by the 19th Brigade in position between Jenlain and Bry, and the cavalry on the outer flank.

General French crossed the Belgian frontier into France when he retired to the position, already reconnoitred, resting on Maubeuge.

This town is situated on both banks of the river Sambre, and is protected by a fortress of the first class. From the statement of a refugee, it would seem Maubeuge can show evidence that the German attack on France had long been premeditated. All the German heavy artillery, he says, was placed on platforms of concrete built on sites carefully selected by private individuals some years ago as the foundation of factories which were never completed.

Fighting, as Sir John tells us, continued on Saturday night, the 22nd, and early on Sunday morning along the whole of the British lines, which were unsupported by the French troops. Mons fell into the hands of the enemy, who were piercing our extreme left, but a cavalry attack on their flank under the direction of General de Lisle checked the further advance of the Germans, and by a tactical feat of great skill, but not without severe losses, Sir John French effected a successful retirement by Sunday night, August 23.

Of the achievements of the three regiments of General de Lisle's command, most is known of the doings of the 9th Lancers, but both the 4th Royal Irish Dragoon Guards and the 18th (Queen Mary's Own) Hussars covered themselves with glory.

The brigade commenced operations in Belgian territory towards Namur, in its own allotted zone. A carefully organised and extensive system of reconnoitring detachments was instituted. Officers' patrols were pushed forward, supported by contact troops. The patrols were also assisted by motor scouts. There was also a concentrated group of squadrons, with two batteries of Royal Horse Artillery, which moved out to meet the enemy at break of day.

Information came to hand of the artillery positions of the Germans, and of preparations being made by them for a general advance. The cavalry field guns were early engaged in operations against the enemy's cavalry, followed later by a *mêlée*, in which the German dragoons got much the worst of it. Fighting took place practically every day, as the British troops were compelled to fall back. The German cavalry were sought for and engaged, in the hope that the enemy's artillery might be captured. There was a fixed desire on the part of our men to get hold of the guns which have played such havoc with shrapnel. A wounded cavalryman says that they have "knocked the stuffing out of the German cavalry."

He says:

At first they came for us, and we put case shot into them at

500 yards, and then dismounted squadrons, and stopped their advance with the rifle, throwing them into confusion. We then mounted and rode straight at them. They opened out and let us ride through them, and it was then we emptied their saddles. They don't appear to like personal encounter. Some were dragged from their seats and pegged with the lance. They don't come for us now, and directly we see them we make for them. We have galloped for a mile to get at them. Once they drew us on to the fire of their infantry. We were only 200 yards away when they fired on us, but we were going too fast for them to hit us.

Our echelons came up into line at the time, and we spread out as we met them hand to hand. Many surrendered without fighting, and those that made off came under the fire of our guns. The German cavalry have excellent mounts, and the horses are well trained. Somehow the men haven't got the same grit as our chaps. When they hear our yell and see our swords they turn pale, and want to be off. If it wasn't for their officers I believe they'd never face us.

The Rev. Owen Spencer Watkins, who was one of the chaplains attached to a Field Ambulance of the British Expeditionary Forces, contributed to the *Methodist Recorder* a story of the retreat with the army from Mons to Paris in care of the wounded. We have ventured to quote from Mr. Watkins's article a few passages:—He left Dublin on August 16 and embarked on the transport *City of Benares*, which carried, besides himself, three Anglican and one Roman Catholic chaplain. During a voyage of forty-eight hours, they were "convoyed" from Ireland to Land's End by British men-of-war, and through the English Channel by French warships. At Land's End the British ship that had been watching over them passed within hailing distance, and the "bluejackets" crowded to the ship's side shouting their good wishes, to which the men on the outgoing boat responded with ringing cheers.

After a train journey from Havre of twenty hours, they reached Valenciennes on Sunday morning, August 23. Mr. Watkins said:

With as little delay as possible we detrained, for we were told the great fight at Mons had already started, and we were urgently needed in the fighting line. Then followed a twenty miles' march, almost without a halt, through villages where the population received us with enthusiasm—showered flowers upon us as we passed, pressed gifts of fruit, wine, cider, tea, and coffee upon the troops, whilst our men, to show their gratitude, shouted '*Vive la France,*' chanted the *Marseillaise*, and cheered until they were hoarse. Then the dark and sleeping villages were suddenly awakened by the tramp of men. The troops were now marching doggedly and silently, the monotonous tramp, tramp almost sent me to sleep in the saddle, and would have done so but for the aching of bones and muscles which for long had been unaccustomed to so many hours on horseback.

Towards the morning of August 24 we halted in the little town of Bavai, and bivouacked in the main square. Here we found a Red Cross Hospital in charge of a priest and a few sisters, and in it were already some of our men; one, a man of the Dorset Regiment, was apparently dying of pneumonia; another, a Royal Engineer, smashed in a motor accident, had just died, and, at the request of the Sisters, Mr. Winnifrith, the Church of England Chaplain, held a little service, where he lay in the mortuary. Then, fully dressed, we threw ourselves down on vacant beds in one of the wards and snatched a couple of hours' sleep.

We wakened just after dawn on August 25 to the sound of heavy firing, and without waiting even for breakfast we at once moved off. Early in our march we learned from a staff officer, who passed us at the gallop, that the British had fallen back, and were now holding the line of the Mons Canal, and that the odds against them were simply overwhelming. He urged us to push on, as there was a shortage of ambulances, and the casualty list was already very heavy. Shortly after we crossed the Belgian frontier, and there were met by the transport of our division (the 5th) returning into France. As we urged forward our weary men and horses, our progress was constantly impeded by pathetic crowds of terror-stricken refugees—women, children, old men—coming along the road in droves, carrying their few valuables on their backs, weeping piteously, some dropping exhausted by the roadside, and all telling heart-rending stories of homes in flames, and some of outrages which made the blood run cold, and caused men to set their lips tight and talk in undertones of the revenge they hoped to take. I cannot describe it; it will not bear thinking about; but it has left a mark on our hearts and memories which nothing can efface.

101

The desperate character of the fighting at Mons is admitted by every survivor of that fierce struggle. Those who had also served in the Boer War say there never was any fighting in South Africa to compare with it. A sergeant gunner of the Royal Field Artillery, wounded in the jaw at Tournai, stated that he was on a flank with his gun and fired about sixty rounds in forty minutes.

> We wanted support and could not get it. It was about 500 English trying to save a flank attack, against, honestly I should say, 10,000. As fast as you shot them down, more came. But for their aeroplanes they would be useless. I was firing for one hour at from 1,500 yards down to 700 yards.

Driver W. Moore, also of the Royal Field Artillery, wrote:—

> It was Sunday night, August 23, when we saw the enemy. We were ready for action, but were lying down to have a rest, when orders came to stand at our posts. It was about four a.m. on Monday when we started to fire; we were at it all day till six p.m., when we started to advance. Then the bugle sounded the charge, and the cavalry and infantry charged like madmen at the enemy; then the enemy fell back about forty miles, so we held at bay till Wednesday, when the enemy was reinforced. Then they came on to Mons, and by that time we had every man, woman, and child out of the town.... We were situated on a hill in a cornfield and we could see all over the country. It was about three p.m., and we started to let them have a welcome by blowing up two of their batteries in about five minutes; then the infantry let go, and then the battle was in full swing.
>
> In the middle of the battle a driver got wounded and asked to see the colours before he died, and he was told by an officer that the guns were his colours. He replied, "Tell the drivers to keep their eyes on their guns, because if we lose our guns we lose our colours."
>
> Just then the infantry had to retire, and the gunners had to leave their guns, but the drivers were so proud of their guns that they went and got them out, and we retired to St. Quentin. We had a roll-call, and only ten were left out of my battery. This was the battle in which poor Winchester (an old Cornwall boy) lost his life in trying to get the guns away.

When the order came to retire it was received by a disappointed force. Such a one was a private in the Middlesex Regiment, who wrote as follows:—

> It was somewhere in the neighbourhood of Mons, I believe, that we got our first chance. We had been marching for days with hardly any sleep. When we took up our position the Germans were nearer than we thought, because we had only just settled down to get some rest when there came the blinding glare of the searchlight. This went away almost as suddenly as it appeared, and it was followed by a perfect hail of bullets. We lost a good many in the fight, but we were all bitterly disappointed when we got the order to retire. I got a couple of bullets through my leg, but I hope it won't be long before I get back again. We never got near enough to use our bayonets. I only wish we had done. Talk about civilised warfare! Don't you believe it. The Germans are perfect fiends.

We have already given the experiences of some of the West Kents, who were in the thick of the fighting from the beginning. The following is an account by another man in this regiment, who said:—

> We were in a scrubby position just outside Mons from Saturday afternoon till Monday morning. After four hours of action each of our six big guns was put out of action. Either the gunners were killed or wounded, or the guns themselves damaged. For the rest of the time—that is, until Monday morning, when we retired—we had to stick the German fire without being able to retaliate. It was bad enough to stand this incessant banging away, but it made it worse not to be able to reply.
>
> All day Sunday and all Sunday night the Germans continued to shrapnel us. At night it was just hellish. We had constructed some entrenchment, but it didn't afford much cover, and our losses were very heavy. On Monday we received the order to retire to the south of the town, and some hours later, when the roll-call was called, it was found that we had 300 dead alone, including four officers.
>
> Then an extraordinary thing happened. Me and some of my pals began to dance. We were just dancing for joy at having escaped with our skins, and to forget the things we'd seen a bit, when bang! and there came a shell from the blue, which burst and got, I should think, quite twenty of us.
>
> That's how some of us got wounded, as we thought we had

escaped. Then another half-dozen of us got wounded this way. Some of our boys went down a street near by, and found a basin and some water, and were washing their hands and faces when another shell burst above them and laid most of them out.

What happened to us happened to the Gloucesters. Their guns, too, were put out of action, and, like us, they had to stand the shell-fire for hours and hours before they were told to retire. What we would have done without our second in command I don't know.

During the Sunday firing he got hit in the head. He had two wounds through the cap in the front and one or two behind, and lost a lot of blood. Two of our fellows helped to bind up his head, and offered to carry him back, but he said, 'It isn't so bad. I'll be all right soon.' Despite his wounds and loss of blood, he carried on until we retired on Monday. Then, I think, they took him off to hospital.

Some further battle stories from wounded men relate to the fighting round Mons. One of the Cheshires said:—

Our chaps were also badly cut up. Apart from the wounded, several men got concussion of the brain by the mere explosions. It was awful! Under the cover of their murderous artillery fire, the German infantry advanced to within three and five hundred yards of our position. With that we were given the order to fix bayonets, and stood up for the charge. That did it for the German infantry! They turned tail and ran for their lives.

Our captain cried out, 'Now you've got 'em, men!' But we hadn't. Their artillery begins with that to fire more hellish than ever, and before you could almost think what to do, fresh lots of the 'sausages' came along, and we had to beat a retreat.

During the retreat one of our sergeants was wounded and fell. With that our captain runs back and tries to lift him. As he was doing so he was struck in the foot, and fell over. We thought he was done for, but he scrambles up and drags the sergeant along until a couple of us chaps goes out to help 'em in.

How a number of British troops made a dash in the night to save some women and children from the Germans was told by Lance-corporal Tanner, of the 2nd Oxfordshire and Bucks Light Infantry:

On Sunday week the regiment arrived at Mons. We took up

our position in the trenches, and fought for some time. In the evening the order came to retire, and we marched back to Condé, with the intention of billeting for the night, and having a rest. Suddenly, about midnight, we were ordered out, and set off to march to the village of Douai, some miles away, as news had reached us that the Germans were slaughtering the natives there.

It was a thrilling march in the darkness, across the unfamiliar country. We were liable to be attacked at any moment, of course, but everyone was keen on saving the women and children, and hurried on. We kept the sharpest look-out on all sides, but saw nothing of the enemy.

When we reached Douai a number of the inhabitants rushed out to meet us. They were overjoyed to see us, and speedily told what the Germans had done. They had killed a number of women and children. With fixed bayonets we advanced into the village, and we saw signs all around us of the cruelty of the enemy.

Private R. Wills, of the Highland Light Infantry, who also took part in the march to the village, here continued the story:

We found that most of the Germans had not waited for our arrival, and there were only a few left in the place. However, we made sure that none remained there.

We started a house-to-house search. Our men went into all the houses, and every now and then they found one or two of the enemy hiding in a corner or upstairs. Many of them surrendered at once, others did not.

When we had cleared the village, some of us lay down on the pavements, and snatched an hour's sleep. At 3.30 we marched away again, having rid the place of the enemy, and, getting back to camp, were glad to turn in.

A gunner of the Lancashire Fusiliers, who was injured by the overturning of his gun, gave his experiences of fighting for seventy-three hours in the neighbourhood of Mons. He spoke of the surprise of some Germans who, while they were being shelled, suddenly received a bayonet charge from a body of men the advance of whom they had not observed as they had crept up under cover. The enemy quickly retired, having lost about 250 men. The gunner expressed a poor opinion of the Germans as shots, who "are frightened of the bayonet, and when charged run faster than our men can pursue them," but he praised their artillery. Speaking of the strength of the Germans, he said there were nine of them to every Englishman. As fast as they were killed, others replaced them, but they succeeded in reducing their numbers. The fusiliers retired to Donicourt, and on ascending a hill the gunner was so injured as to be unable to move; he was fortunately picked up by a Frenchman, who conveyed him to the hospital at St. Quentin. The Germans have a trick of disabling the wounded from using rifles again by injuring their wrists, jamming them on the ground by the butts of their weapons.

It is not an uncommon thing for men to get separated from their regiments; it is often the fate of those who are reported missing or lost. At Mons the enemy cut off some of the Somerset Light Infantry, most of whom hid themselves until dark, and then throwing away their rifles managed to crawl between the German pickets. They did not, however, succeed in regaining their regiments, but made their way to the homes of peasants, who supplied them with civilian clothes. They had some narrow escapes from being arrested for German spies, as they could speak no French, but eventually they reached Boulogne, where they obtained a pass to England and were able to rejoin their depot.

The following stories also illustrate the perils attending missing troops and their endeavours to regain the British lines. The first, from a letter of a non-commissioned officer of dragoons, tells of the adventures of himself and a companion who lost their regiment on the Belgian frontier:—

> We struck, after a very sharp and dangerous engagement, a tiny village, where the priest was absolutely an angel, and gave us—the four who got there—food, shelter, and clothing, and hid a corporal and myself in an old belfry, and a couple of infantry-men, wounded at Mons, in a secret crypt. Since then much has happened. A veterinary officer and sergeant of hussars, who had lost their way and could not speak a word of French, happened to hit the next village, and an old hawker managed to induce them by signs to follow him to our lair.
> "What was he to do?" asked the officer. "Had the *Uhlans* gone west or east? Should they disguise and risk it, or face the certainty of being made prisoners if caught in uniform?" We settled it by a compromise, which has so far answered, for no

Uhlans have appeared to molest us on the road, though we saw on the skyline about thirty trotting in the direction of ——. If they saw us through their field-glasses we should only appear to them as market gardeners or agricultural labourers, taking in a heavy load of potatoes, turnips, and garden produce, and suitably attired.

All our kit and arms had been sent on in advance in a donkey-cart, driven by an old woman, and in such a broken-down condition that even a keen-eyed Prussian would not have detected the false bottom we spent a day in making for the purpose of secreting government property. The old *curé* roared with laughter at the ingenuity of the veterinary officer who designed the dodge and helped to make it.

The carrier's wagon, in which we drove two horses, was now flanked by two pack horses with saddlebags on each horse (we had four altogether), stuffed with tomatoes and artichokes, on a French country saddle. I rode one and the officer rode the other. Peasants we met told us that all along the —— road small parties of strangers had been passing whom they thought must be soldiers, but they were not dressed in uniform. So it seems clear that many of our men have been cut off from their units and are moving towards the coast.

Our first night after leaving —— was at a village where there was a delicious running stream, and we bathed to our hearts' content in a secluded bend away from the public gaze. The people were shy and seemed alarmed, so the officer showed them a letter from our dear old friend the priest, which served as an informal passport during our journey.

The *Uhlans* had been there and paid for some food, cleared the chairs away from the church and turned it into a stable, and although the people had shown them every civility the Germans threw manure into the holy water stoup, smashed the head of the blessed Virgin statue, and wilfully disfigured the shrine of St. Louis de France in whose honour a small chapel had been erected. There were no houses damaged, and it is a curious fact that in this particular instance the *Uhlans* had behaved as religious maniacs of a peculiarly disgusting type, breaking the glass of the church windows, tearing the lace altar frontal, breaking every candlestick upon the altar, and using the vestments of the priest for horse-rubbers.

The other account, like the first, communicated to the *Daily Telegraph*, is from Lieutenant F.V. Drake, of the 11th Hussars, and tells of his escape after the fighting at Mons. Speaking of the retiring movement, he says:—

After six days I was left with thirty-six men to hold the Germans back while the others got away; but we were surrounded by a brigade of German cavalry. First of all we tried to get across country, and were caught up in barbed wire, and they turned two machine guns on us. They killed a lot of horses, but not many men. We then fought our way on to the road which leads into the village of Honcourt. The village was held by the Germans, and barricaded. We were being shot at from behind and in front, and there was barbed wire on both sides of the road.

We charged the barricade. My horse was shot about 200 yards before I got to the barricade, and I was stunned a bit. When I got up again I found all the other fellows swarming on the barricade. I "joined in the hunt," and eight others and I eventually got out of the village on foot into a wood, where I divided the men into twos, and told them the direction in which to go and left them, telling each pair to hide in different parts of the wood.

We spent two days and two nights in that wood, with the Germans absolutely round us; they were so near, in fact, that we could hear every word they said. Leaving the wood by night, we pushed on to where we heard the English were at Cambrai; but when we got there we found they had left the day before. We then hid in a wine cellar, and the Germans came and burnt down the house above us. We, however, escaped through a ventilator. We crawled out through the kitchen garden and hid in some wheat sheaves for the rest of that day, and at night we moved south, where we heard firing going on.

We averaged every night about twenty-five kilometres. We always marched by compass, and always went absolutely plumb straight across country. Each day we hid in henhouses, outbuildings, or wherever we could, and marched by night. We found the inhabitants extremely nice. Wherever possible they gave us food—if the Germans had not taken it all.

Later we secured a motorcar, and proceeded towards St. Pol, but when we had proceeded about halfway we found a German sentry outside a house. We raced past him, and he fired a shot or two, but missed us, and we got safely through the village. Boulogne was eventually reached without further adventure.

One of the most graphic descriptions of the five days' fighting at Mons is contained in a letter from a wounded Gordon Highlander. He relates that on Sunday, August 23, his regiment rose at 4 a.m., and marching out 1,100 strong took up ground on the extreme left flank of the British force and made good trenches, which apparently was the reason that they escaped with comparatively few casualties.

Later in the day a hellish tornado of shell swept over us, and with this introduction to war we received our baptism of fire. We were lining the Mons road, and immediately in our front and to our rear were woods. In the rear wood was stationed a battery of R.F.A."

The German artillery he spoke of as wonderful, and most of those do who have had experience of it. The first shot generally found them, as if the ranges had been carefully taken beforehand. But the British gunners were better, and they hammered and battered the Germans all the day long.

They were at least three to our one, and our artillery could not be in fifty places at once, so we just had to stick it. The German infantry are bad skirmishers and rotten shots, and they were simply mowed down in batches by our chaps. They came in companies of, I should say, 150 men in file five deep, and we simply rained bullets at them the live-long day. At about five p.m. the Germans in the left front of us retired, and we saw no more of them.

The Royal Irish Regiment had had an awful smashing earlier on, as also had the Middlesex, and our company were ordered to go along the road as reinforcements. The one and a half mile seemed a thousand. Stormed at all the way, we kept on, and no one was hit until we came to a white house which stood in a clearing. Immediately the officer passed the gap hell was let loose on us, but we got across safely, and I was the only one wounded, and that was with a ricochet shrapnel bullet in the right knee.

I knew nothing about it until an hour after, when I had it pointed out to me. I dug it out with a knife. We passed dead civilians, some women, and a little boy with his thigh shattered by a bullet. Poor wee fellow. He lay all the time on his face, and some man of the Irish was looking after him, and trying to make him comfortable. The devils shelled the hospital and killed the wounded, despite a huge Red Cross flag flying over it.

When we got to the Royal Irish Regiment's trenches the scene was terrible. They were having dinner when the Germans opened on them, and their dead and wounded were lying all around. Beyond a go at some German cavalry, the day drew in, and darkness saw us on the retreat. The regiment lost one officer and one man dead, one officer and some men severely wounded.

We kept up this sort of game (fighting by day and retiring by night) until we got to Cambrai, on Tuesday night. I dare not mention that place and close my eyes. God, it was awful. Avalanche followed avalanche of fresh German troops, but the boys stuck to it, and we managed to retire to Ham without any molestation. Cambrai was the biggest battle fought. Out of all the glorious regiment of 1,100 men only five officers and 170 of the men answered the roll-call next day. Thank God, I was one of them.

Of course, there may be a number who got separated from the battalion through various causes, and some wounded who escaped. I hope so, because of the heavy hearts at home. I saw the South Lanes, and they were terribly cut up, only a remnant left of the regiment.

Operations of the French troops at this date are described by the Paris correspondent of the *Daily Telegraph*, who stated that:—

Incursions of the German cavalry forces had been made into the district of Valenciennes, Lille, and Douai, in the North of France, with the result that they got a bad reception and were cut up. The raid was carried out by three separate columns, one of which started in the direction of Lille, the second swept around Valenciennes, and the third advanced in the direction of Cambrai.

The first column crossed the frontier line and headed for Lille, but before it got to Lille it had a sharp encounter with the French. The column fell back, and finally moved on towards Douai. In its zigzag course it left a number of prisoners.

The second cavalry column, which was more important, crossed the French frontier on Monday evening, August 24. Faithful to their cruel practice, they compelled, under threat of instant shooting, a number of women and children to walk in front of them. Towards morning a battery of artillery, which had taken position and was concealed in a wood, opened fire on the enemy and caused great slaughter.

Eye-witnesses of the action relate that the column was entirely broken up. The few survivors who escaped fled, but were captured.

The British made a stout resistance in their position against Maubeuge, while the rest of the forces at Mons fell back. The pressure from the Germans increased in severity. Not only were their numbers vastly superior to ours, but they were said to comprise a body of their best men, animated with a determination to crush our lines. In those places where the strain was felt to be overpowering, especially on the left, some further support was given by our cavalry, who did splendid service in checking the enemy's advance. When a battery of heavy German guns was playing havoc with our trenches, and the force of our artillery was beginning to lose effect, an order was given to the 9th Lancers to put the enemy's guns out of action, and under a terrific storm of shell and shrapnel the order was carried out by a daring cavalry charge. The French were still retiring, and it was now evident that the position occupied by our troops was without sufficient advantage to enable them to make a further stand against the foe with any prospect of success. Dangerous as the operation was, Sir John French decided to retire, and to meet the Germans in what proved to be a most deadly conflict.

Sir John French continues the story of his retirement, and deals with the events of August 25, in the following section of his despatch:—

The French were still retiring, and I had no support except such as was afforded by the Fortress of Maubeuge; and the determined attempts of the enemy to get round my left flank assured me that it was his intention to hem me against that place and surround me. I felt that not a moment must be lost in retiring to another position.

I had every reason to believe that the enemy's forces were somewhat exhausted, and I knew that they had suffered heavy losses.

I hoped therefore that his pursuit would not be too vigorous to prevent me effecting my object.

The operation, however, was full of danger and difficulty, not only owing to the very superior force in my front, but also to the exhaustion of the troops.

The retirement was recommenced in the early morning of the 25th to a position in the neighbourhood of Le Cateau, and rearguards were ordered to be clear of the Maubeuge—Bavai—Eth Road by 5.30 a.m.

Two cavalry brigades, with the divisional cavalry of the Second Corps, covered the movement of the Second Corps. The remainder of the cavalry division with the 19th Brigade, the whole under the command of General Allenby, covered the west flank.

The 4th Division commenced its detrainment at Le Cateau on Sunday, the 23rd, and by the morning of the 25th eleven battalions and a brigade of artillery with divisional staff were available for service.

I ordered General Snow to move out to take up a position with his right south of Solesmes, his left resting on the Cambrai—Le Cateau Road south of La Chaprie. In this position the division rendered great help to the effective retirement of the Second and First Corps to the new position.

Although the troops had been ordered to occupy the Cambrai—Le Cateau—Landrecies position, and the ground had, during the 25th, been partially prepared and entrenched, I had grave doubts—owing to the information I received as to the accumulating strength of the enemy against me—as to the wisdom of standing there to fight.

Having regard to the continued retirement of the French on my right, my exposed left flank, the tendency of the enemy's western corps (II.) to envelop me, and, more than all, the exhausted condition of the troops, I determined to make a great effort to continue the retreat till I could put some substantial obstacle, such as the Somme or the Oise, between my troops and the enemy, and afford the former some opportunity of rest and reorganisation. Orders were, therefore, sent to the corps commanders to continue their retreat as soon as they possibly could towards the general line Vermand—St. Quentin—Ribemont.

The cavalry, under General Allenby, were ordered to cover the retirement.

Throughout the 25th and far into the evening, the First Corps continued its march on Landrecies, following the road along the eastern border of the Forêt de Mormal, and arrived at Landrecies about 10 o'clock. I had intended that the corps should come further west so as to fill up the gap between Le Cateau and Landrecies, but the men were exhausted and could not get further in without rest.

The enemy, however, would not allow them this rest, and about 9.30 p.m. a report was received that the 4th Guards Brigade in Landrecies was heavily attacked by troops of the 9th German Army Corps who were coming through the forest on the north of the town. This brigade fought most gallantly and caused the enemy to suffer tremendous loss in issuing from the forest into the narrow streets of the town. This loss has been estimated from reliable sources at from 700 to 1,000. At the same time information reached me from Sir Douglas Haig that his 1st Division was also heavily engaged south and east of Maroilles. I sent urgent messages to the commander of the two French Reserve Divisions on my right to come up to the assistance of the First Corps, which they eventually did. Partly owing to this assistance, but mainly to the skilful manner in which Sir Douglas Haig extricated his corps from an exceptionally difficult position in the darkness of the night, they were able at dawn to resume their march south towards Wassigny on Guise.

By about 6 p.m. the Second Corps had got into position with their right on Le Cateau, their left in the neighbourhood of Caudry, and the line of defence was continued thence by the 4th Division towards Seranvillers, the left being thrown back.

A *communiqué* issued by the French War Office on September 1 explains the forced retirement of the French from their position near Givet, and the consequent withdrawal of our troops from Cateau and Cambrai on August 25. The prompt action of the British troops at this very critical stage undoubtedly saved the French from disaster:—

The Franco-British forces were originally engaged in the region of Dinant, Charleroi, and Mons. Some partial checks were suffered, and the forcing of the Meuse by the Germans near Givet on our flank obliged our troops to fall back, the Germans all the time trying to approach by the west.

In these circumstances our British Allies, attacked by superi-
or numbers in Cateau and Cambrai, had to retire towards the
south when we were operating in the region of Avesnes and
Chimay. The retreating movement continued during the following days, although a general battle took place during its
progress. This engagement was notable for an important success
on our right, where we threw back the Prussian Guard and the
Tenth Corps on to the Oise.

As a set-off to this, and because of the progress of the right German wing, where our adversaries concentrated the finest army
corps, we had to record a new withdrawing movement.

To sum up, on our right, after partial checks, we had taken the
offensive, and the enemy was retreating before us. In the centre
we had alternative successes and checks, but a general battle was
again in progress. The *moral* of the Allies' troops continued to be
extremely good in spite of their losses, which were made good
from the depots.

We will now quote again from the narrative of the Rev. Owen
Spencer Watkins, whose courage was worthy of the army to which he
was attached. He had a narrow escape of being taken prisoner. After
leaving Villars Sal he learnt from a motor-cyclist who passed them that
the Germans had entered on one side of the village as they went out
of the other. At Villersan they halted.

Horses and men, transport and guns, an endless procession they
passed, blackened with grime, bearing evident signs of the past
few days of fighting. And behind were the infantry still fighting a rearguard action. But the men were in good spirits; they
were retreating, but this was not a defeated army. . . . The town
of Cambrai was now in sight, and we were told that just beyond it, at a place called Le Cateau, was a position we could
hold, and here we should entrench and make a stand. . . . Once
I passed through a division of French cavalry, who greeted me
most courteously, and were very curious to know exactly what
my duties with the army were. A great contrast they presented
to our khaki-clad troops in their blue and red and gold, but it
struck me that such finery was hardly likely to be so serviceable
as our more sombre khaki.

On the morning of Wednesday, August 26, after four hours'

sleep in the rain, I was awakened by the sound of heavy guns, and rose from my bed of straw to realise that the Battle of Le Cateau had begun. As I had slept booted and spurred, no time was wasted in toilet, and I was able at once to ride off to the scene of action, whilst the ambulance wagons and stretcher-bearers were making ready to do likewise. I visited the infantry lining their trenches, but they had not yet come into action. As I talked with them I little thought how many hundreds of these lads of the 14th Infantry Brigade (Manchesters, Suffolks, Duke of Cornwall's Light Infantry, and East Surreys) would be lying low before the end of day.

Later I was for a while with the 108th Heavy Battery, whose guns were masked with corn-sheaves to hide them from the German aeroplane, and who even, whilst I was with them, did terrible execution. The great 60-pounder shells were burst with wonderful precision and deadly effect, and before the day was over this battery alone had completely exterminated two batteries of German artillery. My next move was to the 15th Brigade Royal Field Artillery, which had just come into action. The story of these batteries is one of the most moving and heroic in the war, and perhaps some day it will be fully told. The losses amongst both men and horses were appalling, yet still they worked their guns. In one battery only a junior officer and one man was left, but between them they still contrived to keep the gun in action.

Now the battle was in full swing, the noise was deafening; the whole can only be realised by one who has himself passed through a similar experience—I cannot describe it.

. . . The casualties were pouring in upon us now, and the worst cases still lay in the trenches, from which they could not be moved until the fire slackened, or darkness came. The injured men told of brave and dogged fighting in the trenches, of an opposing host that seemed without number, of casualties so numerous that they seemed to us an exaggeration, and later of trenches that were being enfiladed by German shrapnel. Evidently the French, who, we understood, were on our flank, had been late in arriving, or else they had retreated, leaving our flank exposed. By this time other batteries were taking up their positions in our vicinity, and it soon became evident that the position was becoming impossible for a dressing station.

But how to move? that was the question; for we had far more wounded than it was possible to carry in our ambulance wagons. So we sorted out all who were able to hop, or walk, or be helped along by comrades, and they were told that they must walk to Busigny as best they could. Meanwhile the operating tents were being pulled down and packed upon the wagons, and as the last were being loaded shell was bursting over our camp. To me was delegated the task of shepherding the wounded who were walking, and seeing them safe to Busigny railway station, where it was hoped they would get a train to take them down country. I never want such a task again.

Up and down that road I galloped, urging one poor fellow to hop faster, expostulating with another who, seated by the roadside, declared he could go no further, and that to fall into the hands of the Germans would be no worse than the agony he endured as he walked. At last I came across a farmer's cart, and taking the law into my own hands, commandeered it, and made the man come back with me and pick up all who could walk no more. Time and again there would be a burst of shrapnel in the road, but as far as I could see nobody was injured. Just off the road the cavalry were at work doing their best to guard our flank as we retreated—for now I learned we were in full retreat—and amongst them the casualties were heavy. Such as we could reach we carried with us. At last, to my infinite relief, Busigny was reached, and I was relieved of my charge.

At Le Cateau the 5th Division lost probably more heavily than any other portion of the British Forces. It was entirely due to the splendid generalship of Sir Horace Smith-Dorrien that we had not to record a great disaster; ever since then we had been in retreat, but it was not a beaten or even a seriously discouraged army.

Fighting on this day is described by some who were present at the battle. The following related to the Royal Dublin Fusiliers:—

Captain Trigona said that on August 26 the main body of the Allies was in the district of Mons, and in the direction of Cambrai his battalion formed a portion of the rearguard, and were continually being harassed by the enemy. An order, which they should have received to retire, miscarried. This, in his opinion, was due to despatch riders falling into the hands of the enemy.

The regiment was left unsupported, and an overwhelming body of the enemy attacking them, they were obliged to retreat. The Germans moved forward in dark, thick masses, and the British rifle did terrible havoc among their closely-packed ranks. The enemy's ranks in places were blotted out by the withering leaden blast which the fusiliers kept up with that dogged determination which has won for the regiment in past wars many golden laurels. The German loss was much greater than ours. This is accounted for by the close formation adopted by the latter.

At one time the regiment had fallen back on a large farmhouse, but a number of shells from the German artillery quickly reduced the building to a heap of debris, and they were forced to evacuate the farm. During the succeeding night Captain Trigona and a small body of men got separated from the other portion of the troops. When daylight broke they found themselves wandering in a country swarming with the enemy's cavalry. They were completely cut off from the Allies' forces, but succeeded in reaching a French village without being molested by the Germans. They were received with every kindness by the villagers. Food was supplied to the well-nigh famished men, and welcome rest was obtained in barns and farmhouses. After eight days' travelling by night and hiding by day they reached Boulogne.

Another officer, in the Irish Guards, wrote a vivid account of the Titanic struggle in the neighbourhood of Cambrai:—

We had a very bad night on Tuesday, August 25, when our billets were attacked by the Germans, and a situation arose which at one time looked very serious for our brigade. However, we held our own, and simply mowed the Germans down. The doctors counted over 2,000 of their dead outside the town next morning when they were collecting our wounded.

I must say now none of us expected to get away. I, with about thirty men, was given a house to defend which commanded two main streets, and we worked away at it from about 10 p.m. until about 1.30 a.m., when we were called out to join the battalion who were going out to attack the Germans with the bayonet. But when we got to the other side of the town we found they had had enough of it, and gone.

I think I shall never forget that night as long as I live. We all had wonderful escapes, with shrapnel shell bursting continuously, high explosive shells, also; houses burning and falling down from the shell fire; the intermittent rifle fire, with every now and then furious bursts of fire when the Germans attacked.

Our biggest fight so far took place at Landrecies. The Germans attacked us in the town furiously. They brought their guns to within fifty yards of us in the dark on the road, and opened point-blank fire. Our gunners brought up a gun by hand, as no horse could have lived, and knocked at least one of the German guns out first shot. This all at about sixty yards.

Notwithstanding the fury of the engagement, the enemy found opportunities to outrage the non-combatants for their own ends. A private in the King's Own Scottish Borderers related that between Mons and Cambrai he had his Glengarry torn to shreds with shrapnel. Before he was hit he saw from 600 yards' range Belgian women tied to the German guns, and this prevented the Coldstream Guards returning the German fire as they retreated in the neighbourhood of Cambrai.

The following is the description of another eyewitness:—

It was on August 26 that we suffered most. Our little lot was waiting for the Germans in a turnip field. We were lying down, and on they came. We let fly, and numbers of them went down. They cracked at us then with their machine guns, and did us a good deal of damage. We were obliged to retire, but there was an off-and-on fight for at least twelve hours. We would get cover and have a smack at 'em, and with their great numbers and our good shooting we did tumble them over. But, my goodness, the numbers did keep coming on, and we had to go back. Our fellows were falling here and there, principally as results of their machine guns, which were doing nearly all the damage. We did not worry a lot about their rifle fire, which was faulty; but we got them every time.

It was the time that we were having a great slap at a bunch of them that we were really tried. We advanced, and pushed them back, but we were outnumbered again. We fell back, and a crush of us got separated from the rest. There were about sixteen of us, and we found ourselves beyond the German lines. In the morning it was "cut and run for it," for everywhere there were

Germans about. We got to a village and hid, the French people taking every care of us. We concealed our arms, and changed our khaki uniforms for any clothes that we could get. In the day-time we hid in barns, under haystacks, or in the homes of French villagers, who were most kind to us.

At Landrecies the Coldstream Guards put up a heroic defence, said a correspondent to the *Daily Telegraph*, when suddenly attacked by the Germans. The Guard says:

Dealing with the operations which led up to the skirmish, owing to the enemy being five or six times our superior in numbers, and attacking from all quarters fiercely. Sir Douglas Haig had to keep his men on the march almost night and day. We had a rough time of it. Our boys were as lively as crickets, but under fire as cool as you could wish. It was getting dark when we found out that the *Kaiser's* crush were coming through a forest, and we soon found out their game.

It was to cut off our force, who were retiring on to Le Cateau covered by our cavalry. We had not long to wait before they swarmed out of the forest and entered the small town from different directions. But we got them everywhere and stopped them, not a man getting through.

About 200 of us drove them down a street, and didn't the devils squeal when at close quarters. They fell in their scores, and we jumped over them to get at the others. At the corner of the street which led to the principal thoroughfare we came upon a mass of them. At this point we were reinforced from two directions. We were pressed for a time, but they soon lost heart, and we actually had to climb over their dead and wounded, which were heaped up, to get at the others. Then we had to race away to another point where they were hurling their masses at us. Those who did not get back to the forest were knocked over.

It looked at one time as if they would get round us, but they got a surprise packet, for we cleared the town and drove them back. I don't know how many we accounted for, but I saw quite 150 heaped together in one street.

We had to continue our retreat, and had little rest until we got to Compiègne on September 1. Here the brigade had a shaking up. It was the Germans' last desperate attempt to get through. What really happened I hardly know. Never before did the

Guards fight as they did that day. We are having reinforcements, and we shall then have a chance of getting our own back, for when pressed they will not stand up to us.

On August 29 Mr. Asquith in the House of Commons announced a wonderful feat of arms by the British army. It was with reference to the engagement in the neighbourhood of Cambrai—Le Cateau on Wednesday, August 26, which Sir John French described as "the most critical day of all." There must have been at the lowest computation 300,000 German troops (five German army corps, two cavalry divisions, and a reserve corps, with the Guard Cavalry and the 2nd Cavalry Division) opposed to two British army corps and a division. The total strength of our forces cannot have exceeded 100,000 men. In other words, the odds were three to one, and were probably much heavier. Our 2nd Army Corps and 4th Division bore the brunt of the cavalry attack, whilst our 1st Army Corps was attacked on the right and inflicted very heavy loss on the enemy. Our casualties were also heavy. General Joffre, in a message published that morning, had conveyed his congratulations and thanks for the protection so effectively given by our army to the French flank.

CHAPTER 5

Fighting in the Valley of the Meuse

The following extract from Sir John French's first despatch brings it to a conclusion as far as the operations of the British army are concerned:—

> During the fighting on the 24th and 25th the cavalry became a good deal scattered, but by the early morning of the 26th General Allenby had succeeded in concentrating two brigades to the south of Cambrai.
>
> The 4th Division was placed under the orders of the general officer commanding the Second Army Corps.
>
> On the 24th the French Cavalry Corps, consisting of three divisions, under General Sordêt, had been in billets north of Avesnes. On my way back from Bavai, which was my "*Poste de Commandement*" during the fighting of the 23rd and 24th, I visited General Sordêt, and earnestly requested his co-operation and support. He promised to obtain sanction from his army commander to act on my left flank, but said that his horses were too tired to move before the next day. Although he rendered me valuable assistance later on in the course of the retirement, he was unable for the reasons given to afford me any support on the most critical day of all, *viz.*, the 26th.
>
> At daybreak it became apparent that the enemy was throwing the bulk of his strength against the left of the position occupied by the Second Corps and the 4th Division.
>
> At this time the guns of four German army corps were in position against them, and Sir Horace Smith-Dorrien reported to me that he judged it impossible to continue his retirement at daybreak (as ordered) in face of such an attack.

I sent him orders to use his utmost endeavours to break off the action and retire at the earliest possible moment, as it was impossible for me to send him any support, the First Corps being at the moment incapable of movement.

The French cavalry corps, under General Sordêt, was coming up on our left rear early in the morning, and I sent an urgent message to him to do his utmost to come up and support the retirement of my left flank; but owing to the fatigue of his horses he found himself unable to intervene in any way.

There had been no time to entrench the position properly, but the troops showed a magnificent front to the terrible fire which confronted them.

The artillery, although outmatched by at least four to one, made a splendid fight and inflicted heavy losses on their opponents.

At length it became apparent that, if complete annihilation was to be avoided, a retirement must be attempted; and the order was given to commence it about 3.30 p.m. The movement was. covered with the most devoted intrepidity and determination by the artillery, which had itself suffered heavily, and the fine work done by the cavalry in the further retreat from the position assisted materially in the final completion of this most difficult and dangerous operation.

Fortunately the enemy had himself suffered too heavily to engage in an energetic pursuit.

I cannot close the brief account of this glorious stand of the British troops without putting on record my deep appreciation of the valuable services rendered by General Sir Horace Smith-Dorrien.

I say without hesitation that the saving of the left wing of the army under my command on the morning of the 26th August could never have been accomplished unless a commander of rare and unusual coolness, intrepidity, and determination had been present to personally conduct the operation.

The retreat was continued far into the night of the 26th and through the 27th and 28th, on which date the troops halted on the line Noyon—Chauny—La Fère, having then thrown off the weight of the enemy's pursuit.

On the 27th and 28th I was much indebted to General Sordêt and the French Cavalry Division which he commands for materially assisting my retirement and successfully driving back some of the enemy on Cambrai.

General d'Amade also, with the 61st and 62nd French Reserve Divisions, moved down from the neighbourhood of Arras on the enemy's right flank and took much pressure off the rear of the British Forces.

This closes the period covering the heavy fighting which commenced at Mons on Sunday afternoon, 23rd August, and which really constituted a four days' battle.

At this point, therefore, I propose to close the present despatch.

Lord Kitchener pointed out in his first speech to the House of Lords, on August 25, while the battle was still waging, that European fighting causes greater casualties than the campaigns to which we are accustomed in other parts of the world, but in spite of hard marching the British Force was in the best of spirits. The casualties to the British troops were very heavy, but the losses inflicted on the Germans, who were always on the offensive, were enormous.

The battle was beyond all comparison the greatest in which our troops had been engaged; although it is not to be compared in point of duration with the tremendous conflict on the Aisne. No officer or man now with the colours had ever known the sort of warfare as that which was waged on the Belgian and French frontiers.

Correspondents found it difficult to obtain from the French descriptions of the recent hard fighting, and Mr. W. T. Massey, of the *Daily Telegraph* staff, wrote that great care was exercised that wounded should not meet and discuss the situation with civilians. Here and there one finds, he said, a non-commissioned officer or private who has been in the fighting line, but they tell you they really know little of what is going on. A hussar he talked to said he had not been in any serious fighting, but he regarded the "charge" as the principal *rôle* of cavalry, because he admitted that he was frequently within rifle shot of the enemy and had been under fire six times for considerable periods.

The cavalry, the hussar said, had kept the Germans in a state of great activity, for directly a cavalry brigade was on the move the enemy seemed instantly to prepare for battle. Over and over again our cavalry would change direction and halt to dig trenches which were never meant to be occupied. The Germans did the same, and tired infantry were continually kept on the move. This hussar described the German field uniform as very difficult to pick up at long ranges, even with field glasses. The French uniform was a much easier target, and khaki did not blend very well with the green of the French landscape.

He had a long talk with a civilian who had been in close touch with one French army corps during the battles in the valley of the Meuse. All through, he was told, it had been a case of fighting against odds, but often bravery and dash overbore superior numbers and caused the German advance to be stayed while a pushed-back line was being strengthened. For instance, at Marville, a French force of 5,000 men of all arms of the 2nd Army Corps not merely stemmed the strong German tide, but rolled back a force of 20,000 men from point to point continuously for twelve hours, and it was not until there was a risk of the French losing touch with their supports that they retired.

All down the Meuse the French destroyed the bridges; this informant said thirty-three bridges had been blown up, and he was given a vivid picture of one of the scenes which followed the destruction of the means of crossing the river. This was at Charleville, an important position on the Meuse, quite close to the fortified town of Mézières, and within a field gun's call from Sedan. Here the French tactics of Sedan were reversed. The *trou* of Sedan is engraven on the memory of every French soldier, and the danger of being caught in a hollow is ever present to officers. The Germans, bound up by military history, and confident that what happened in 1870 would occur again, fell into a trap which cost them dear.

He said:

Last Tuesday (August 25), the French decided to evacuate Charleville, and sent round to the inhabitants to clear out. Trains took away many civilians, but a number had to travel on foot, and the roads in the early morning were covered with a long line of stragglers toiling under the burden of the few household treasures they had saved from the threatened destruction.

As the civil population left, a small party of French riflemen marched into the town to play a part worthy of the traditions of their army. I did not realise until the action developed that their duty involved enormous risk and that it was almost in the nature of a forlorn hope. They were sent to occupy a few houses which controlled the roads through the town, and though these houses were marked out to the French artillery when the guns began to bark, the lives of the members of this party were always in danger. If any survive they will have earned any decoration for bravery, for their ambush assisted in the complete destruction of a considerable German force of cavalry and infantry.

Around Charleville is a semi-circular sweep of hills. On these the French artillery was posted, the guns being dug in and hidden from the eyes of German scouts. The Germans were seen coming over the three bridges leading into the town. They were not opposed for a long time, and their numbers grew rapidly. Suddenly the three bridges were blown up, and the retreat was cut off. The destruction of the bridges was the signal to the guns on the high ground to begin, while the riflemen in ambush poured a terrible fire into an enemy who had a moment before believed they were occupying a deserted town. They were also raked by an awful fire from half a dozen batteries.

Into all parts of the town, save in the riflemen were doing their country's work, there was a tornado of bursting shells, houses falling into the streets, and clouds of dust rising from the shrapnel bullets as they rained in a pitiless mass upon broken plaster and bricks. In a few minutes—ten minutes, I should say—the town was destroyed, and the whole German force must have been annihilated. I can imagine how completely the Germans were taken by surprise. Directly they got across the bridges they must have thought they had, indeed, got a prize. Charleville had been made the depot for captured German cannon, and in the gun park there were, I am told, ninety-five field guns taken at God knows what sacrifice by the Allies. I saw the guns, but though I cannot vouch for the number, I can say there were very many. Twelve had been added just before the town was evacuated.

Of course, the breech blocks and mechanism had been so burred and damaged that the guns, as they stood, were useless, but the recovery of even useless weapons would give encouragement to an enemy, and, no doubt, many German soldiers were contemplating their restoration to their army when the bursting shells cried out, "Not yet." That scene, so triumphant for French arms, was awful, and I went away before the remnant of the riflemen was collected from the ruined town—that is, if there were any survivors; I devoutly pray there were many—and Charleville and the gun park were left for other German eyes to look upon as an example of what war is.

I asked my informant, who expressed a wish that I would say nothing to give a clue to identification, whether he had seen any German prisoners. He replied, "Yes, a large number. They complain that the transport line is mainly occupied with war material, and that the food supply is neglected. All the enemy's soldiers, they say, are hungry, and some of the men in the firing-lines have been without food for two days. On the other hand, the French soldiers—I have not been with British troops, but have seen their commissariat columns proceeding regularly and quickly backwards and forwards—have always plenty."

As the road from Abbeville to Amiens approaches the latter pictur-esque town, it runs for a considerable distance alongside the railway. Mr. Massey was in the district on Friday afternoon, August 28, and when in the neighbourhood of Picquigny he found the railroad con-gested and the highway almost full of people proceeding south. Here and there, hidden in hedgerows, were files of French territorial infan-try, and dotted over the countryside to the north sentries were vigi-lant. An officer stated that the latest report which had come in warned him that a *Uhlan* patrol was less than six kilometres away, and the presence of the enemy so far south suggested that a bold attempt was being made to cut the railway and destroy the utility of Boulogne as a base. The Germans probably did not know that at this time the British had ceased to employ Boulogne as a port for the disembarkation of men and stores, and that no British troops remained at Boulogne.

The last train that was running out of Boulogne for Amiens was before him, and he knew that little rolling-stock remained at the port. The service both ways had been cut off, but the Boulogne-Folkestone boats were running. While he watched a fast train ran by towards the coast, and succeeding it came four big engines coupled together. Pres-ently one of them returned with two trucks, holding eighty French soldiers, who were deposited on the line, half of them guarding the passenger train and the remainder reinforcing the guards on the line of communications. By and by word was passed along to keep the road clear for troops, and carts pulled on to one side. In a few minutes some khaki-clad soldiers swung round a bend. Their gait showed they were not Britishers, and the *kepi* or *fez* indicated their origin.

They were two companies of French Algerian troops, the "Turcos," as they are called. They advanced rapidly, shuffling along rather than marching, carrying their equipment easily. With them were three ammunition mules, entrenching tools carried in a mule pack, and two light carts. Officers showed their delight at the prospect of getting into touch with the enemy by waving their hands at cheering people, while the rank and file raised their arms, palm of the hand uppermost, and acknowledged the salutations by opening and closing the hand. They were a happy party, and they brushed past the villagers and quickened their pace to get to the point assigned to them.

The villagers were satisfied that the coloured troops would stand till the last man, but there were many of their compatriots moving forward with their families to places more secure. Generally these fugitives were of the farming class, and each of the long, low farm wagons was a tale of tragedy of the war. Weary horses hauled vehicles piled up with household goods. The drivers were mere lads or old men, whose years unfitted them for military service, and packages of all sorts, and perambulators in some cases, occupied one-half of the space, and women and children, seated on hay and straw, the remainder. Nobody seemed to speak; abandoned homes and the fear that all was not well with the army in which their men-folk were serving made them dumb. But if there was panic, nobody showed it, for all met the situation with stolid countenances and were apparently ready to accept what the fates decreed.

Passengers on the train were more alarmed. They, too, had heard that German cavalry were near, and they chafed at the vexatious stoppages every couple of hundred yards. But every move forward was nearer safety, and all seemed pleased that French infantry marched by the side of the train. A progress of a mile an hour for the last three miles satisfied nobody, and when Amiens was reached the summons given to passengers for Paris to change caused some concern. The lines were mainly occupied by troop trains, as they had been for eighteen hours. The French wastage of war has been more than made good in this region.

You meet refugees by the thousand, and a man with a heart of flint would be sorry for them. On every grim visage is written the stern realities of war. Infinite suffering, aye, and splendid courage and patriotism, is lined on every face, and you feel when they pass you by that heroism is shared almost in an equal degree by most civilians and fighting men.

Old Frenchmen, who have left behind them the fortunes they have built; children, who were learning to hope they would follow in worthy footsteps; dames who had earned repose by reason of arduous and thrifty years of activity, and younger women who gloried in husbands' commercial enterprise and success, passed you, not broken people, but a crowd who will have to begin life anew when the scourge of war has ceased scarring the land.

Of all the people moving in advance of the brutal German line, one's sympathies must go out to the women. Mr. Massey continues:

> It has been my good fortune—for though it was a sight which made one feel the terrible penalties inflicted by war, it brought out vividly the nobler side of humanity—to be very near the fighting line in the past two days, and I have watched many a case of women's heroism. It was not the self-denial of Red Cross nurses that impressed me most. To that one is accustomed. But the long procession of weary women, cheerfully encouraging children, hungry and tired and footsore, or with bones aching from the jolting of farm carts, was a picture of splendid courage, which made you understand how a nation becomes resolute in face of war. The women play their part silently and without complaint.
>
> Of the thousands of big-hearted women I have seen during the past sixteen days in France, I need only refer to one. She is an example of the patriotic Frenchwoman of today. I met her at a town which was evacuated, and she was proceeding with a splendid son of France, aged ten, and a delightfully talkative little girl of eight, to a place where her children would be safe from the oppression of an enemy. This cultured lady is the wife of a captain of cavalry who is doing a patriot's work. As she looked back at her home at Longwy she saw a lifetime's treasures burnt, but the sadness of her heart was not betrayed to her children. To them she merely indicated that a gallant father's regiment would see to it that they returned home soon.
>
> Horses and vehicles were required for the country's service, so the mother and children walked through French lines to where they thought they would be safe. They proceeded west, and went through Marville (where "Daddy" was fighting), on to Charleville. Here they rested and waited, not dreaming that a weakened left wing would cause the whole French line to retire and force a reassembling on positions further south. But strategy is left to men in France, and when word was sent round that the inhabitants of Charleville should leave their dwell-

ings, the cavalry officer's wife and children gave up seats in the last south-bound train to old people and trudged over rolling ground for thirty kilometres before they reached a railway-line which still provided a train for civilians.

When I saw this family the mother had not tasted food for three days, and the children did not want to eat while the mother starved. The bright eyes of the boy were not dimmed by the exhaustion of bearing his part in carrying a bag too heavy for his immature shoulders, and it was glorious to see the comfort he was to his mother.

You got a true insight into French patriotism when, instead of hearing complaints of hardships, you were questioned as to the latest news from the battle-line. And if you knew less than mother and boy you forgave the look of pity which followed your answer. You, they thought, should be where the British soldiers were. And this small family, which I watched for eight hours during a dreary progress away from a sternly-fought area, was but a type of thousands of others. Truly war brings out the best, as well as the worst, of humanity.

CHAPTER 6

The French Army on the Oise

The Press Bureau supplied, on September 7, a survey of the activities of the British Expeditionary Army which has, it stated, conformed to the general movement of the French forces and acted in harmony with the strategic conceptions of the French General Staff.

After the battle at Cambrai, on August 26, where the British troops successfully guarded the left flank of the whole line of French armies from a deadly turning attack, supported by enormous force, the 7th French Army came into operation on our left, and, in conjunction with the 5th Army on our right, this greatly relieved our men from the strain and pressure.

The 5th French Army, in particular, on August 29 advanced from the line of the Oise River to meet and counter the German forward movement, and a considerable battle developed to the south of Guise.

In this, the 5th French Army gained a marked and solid success, driving back with heavy loss and in disorder three German Army Corps, the 10th, the Guard, and a reserve corps.

It is believed that the commander of the 10th German Corps was among those killed.

In spite of this success, however, and all the benefits which flowed from it, the general retirement to the south continued, and the German armies, seeking persistently after the British troops, remained in practically continuous contact with our rearguards.

Sir John French's despatch of September 17 describes the operations of the British Forces on August 28 and 29:—

On that evening the retirement of the force was followed closely by two of the enemy's cavalry columns, moving southeast from St. Quentin.

The retreat in this part of the field was being covered by the 3rd and 5th Cavalry Brigades. South of the Somme General Gough, with the 3rd Cavalry Brigade, threw back the Uhlans of the Guard with considerable loss.

General Chetwode, with the 5th Cavalry Brigade, encountered the eastern column near Cérizy, moving south. The brigade attacked and routed the column, the leading German regiment suffering very severe casualties and being almost broken up.

The 7th French Army Corps was now in course of being railed up from the south to the east of Amiens. On the 29th it nearly completed its detrainment, and the French 6th Army got into position on my left, its right resting on Roye.

The 5th French Army was behind the line of the Oise, between La Fère and Guise.

The pursuit of the enemy was very vigorous; some five or six German corps were on the Somme, facing the 5th Army on the Oise. At least two corps were advancing towards my front, and were crossing the Somme east and west of Ham. Three or four more German corps were opposing the 6th French Army on my left.

This was the situation at 1 o'clock on the 29th, when I received a visit from General Joffre at my headquarters.

I strongly represented my position to the French commander-in-chief, who was most kind, cordial, and sympathetic, as he has always been. He told me that he had directed the 5th French Army on the Oise to move forward and attack the Germans on the Somme, with a view to checking pursuit. He also told me of the formation of the 6th French Army on my left flank, composed of the 7th Army Corps, four Reserve Divisions, and Sordêt's Corps of cavalry.

I finally arranged with General Joffre to effect a further short retirement towards the line Compiègne—Soissons, promising him, however, to do my utmost to keep always within a day's march of him.

In pursuance of this arrangement the British Forces retired to a position a few miles north of the line Compiègne—Soissons on the 29th.

The right flank of the German Army was now reaching a point which appeared seriously to endanger my line of communications with Havre. I had already evacuated Amiens, into which place a German reserve division was reported to have moved.

Orders were given to change the base to St. Nazaire, and establish an advance base at Le Mans. This operation was well carried out by the Inspector-General of Communications.

In spite of a severe defeat inflicted upon the Guard 10th and Guard Reserve Corps of the German Army by the 1st and 3rd French Corps on the right of the 5th Army, it was not part of General Joffre's plan to pursue this advantage; and a general retirement on to the line of the Marne was ordered, to which the French Forces in the more eastern theatre were directed to conform.

A new army (the 9th) had been formed from three corps in the south by General Joffre, and moved into the space between the right of the 5th and left of the 4th Armies.

Whilst closely adhering to his strategic conception to draw the enemy on at all points until a favourable situation was created from which to assume the offensive. General Joffre found it necessary to modify from day to day the methods by which he sought to attain this object, owing to the development of the enemy's plans and changes in the general situation.

In conformity with the movements of the French Forces, my retirement continued practically from day to day. Although we were not severely pressed by the enemy, rearguard actions took place continually.

On August 30 and 31, the British covering and delaying troops were frequently engaged. In the districts of St. Quentin—Verdun and Ham—Péronne a battle was fought lasting some days. The special correspondent to the *Daily Telegraph* wrote:—

St. Quentin, the scene of the British fight on Sunday, August 30, was ready for evacuation a couple of days previously. On the British right the French force, under the gallant General Pau, scored a distinct success. On Sunday and Monday the Germans were hotly pressed near Guise, and the French, once getting the upper hand, hammered away at the enemy, and completely demoralised them. One German army corps was completely broken and thrown into the Oise, and, being cut off on both sides from their supports, lost fearfully, a remnant withdrawing and leaving enormous numbers of dead, wounded, and prisoners in the valley.

A captain of a French infantry regiment reached the Gare du Nord yesterday, with his left leg shattered by a shell; but the severity of his wound did not prevent him describing the battle of Guise as he saw it. "The Germans who engaged us were," he said, "the *élite* of their army—the 10th Corps and the Imperial Guard—but our troops gave proof of their extreme bravery and of their marvellous dash. They received heroically the German thrust, and very soon took a vigorous offensive, which was crowned with success. The German masses were forced to bend back, and their losses were enormous. I am certain of that. When I fell, the German retreat increased, and our offensive movement claimed victory. But on our left the line was bent back to La Fère, and the offensive could not therefore be persisted in"

The correspondent to the *Daily Telegraph* stated that at St. Quentin, when he retired from Landrecies, General French established himself temporarily in the Lycée Henri-Martin, named after the most patriotic historian of France. The English artillery covered the heights that command the town. It was a repetition of the Battle of Saint Quentin of 1870, with this difference—that the enemy approached the town from another direction. For the space of ten days or so fierce and uninterrupted fighting took place between Saint Quentin, Péronne, and Vervins. A French artillery regiment was at a place called Catelet, between Cambrai and Saint Quentin. However, the German column, in spite of these attacks on both its flanks, one of which was driven back on to Guise a week ago, continued to force its way towards the Oise valley, and General French moved his headquarters first to Noyon, and then to Clermont. The English troops were then deployed all the way between Clermont and Soissons.

On Monday, August 31, the Allies' left was brought round and southwards, their headquarters being at Aumale, where General d'Amade, the hero of the French Morocco campaign, was with his staff.

A very vigorous effort was made by the Germans on September 1, which brought about a sharp action in the neighbourhood of Compiègne. The action was fought principally by the ist British Cavalry Brigade and the 4th Guards Brigade, with a body of German cavalry, preceded by a light scouting column in the forest of Compiègne, and was entirely satisfactory to the British. The German attack, which was most strongly pressed, was not brought to a standstill until much slaughter had been inflicted upon them, and until ten German guns had been captured. The brunt of this creditable affair fell upon our Guards Brigade, who lost in killed and wounded about 300 men.

Another corps of German cavalry advancing on the opposite flank of the column pushed its line to the railway station at Anizy-le-Château, between Laon and Soissons. The enemy, however, found that the railway line had been rendered useless.

We venture to quote the fine account of fighting at Compiègne which was given by a wounded Guardsman in the *Evening News*. In this action ten of the enemy's guns were captured.

> We were in a field when the Germans dropped on us all of a sudden. The first hint we had of their presence was when a battery of guns on the right sang out, dropping shells into a mob of us who were waiting for our turn at the wash tub—the river.
>
> There was no panic as far as I saw, only some of our fellows who hadn't had a wash for a long time said strong things about the Germans for spoiling the best chance we had had for four days.
>
> We all ran to our posts in response to bugles which ran out all along the line, and by the time we all stood to arms the German cavalry came into view in great strength all along the left front.
>
> As soon as they came within range we poured a deadly volley into them, emptying saddles right and left, and they scattered in all directions. Meanwhile their artillery kept working up closer on the front and the right, and a dark cloud of infantry showed out against the sky-line on our front, advancing in a formation rather loose for the Germans.
>
> We opened on them, and they made a fine target for our rifle fire, which was very well supported by our artillery. The fire from our guns was very effective, the range being found with ease, and we could see the shells dropping right into the enemy's ranks.
>
> Here and there their lines began to waver and give way, and

finally they disappeared. Half an hour later more infantry appeared on our right front, but we could not say whether it was the same or another body. This time they were well supported by artillery, machine guns, and strong forces of cavalry on both flanks. All came on at a smart pace with the apparent plan of seizing a hill on our right. At the same moment our cavalry came into view, and then the whole Guards Brigade advanced. It was really a race between the two parties to reach the hill first, but the Germans won easily, owing to their being nearer by half a mile.

As soon as their guns and infantry had taken up a position, the cavalry came along in a huge mass with the intention of riding down the Irish Guards, who were nearest to them. When the shock came it seemed terrific to us in the distance, for the Irishmen didn't recoil in the least, but flung themselves right across the path of the German horsemen.

We could hear the crack of the rifles and see the German horses impaled on the bayonets of the front ranks of the Guardsmen; then the whole force of infantry and cavalry were mixed up in one confused heap like so many pieces from a jigsaw puzzle. Shells from the British and German batteries kept dropping close to the tangled mass of fighting men, and then we saw the German horsemen get clear and take to flight as fast as their horses would carry them. Some had no horses, and they were bayoneted where they stood.

While this was going on there was a confused movement among the German infantry, as though they were going to the assistance of the cavalry, but evidently they did not like the look of things, for they stayed where they were. After this little interruption the whole of the Guards continued their advance, the Coldstreamers leading this time, with the Scots in reserve and the Irish in support.

Taking advantage of the fight between the cavalry and infantry, the German artillery had advanced to a new position, from which they kept up a deadly fire from twelve guns. Our infantry and cavalry advanced simultaneously against this new position, which they carried together in the face of a galling fire.

In the excitement the enemy managed to get away two of their guns, but the remainder fell into our hands. The infantry and cavalry supporting the guns didn't wait for the onslaught of our men, but bolted like mad, pursued by our cavalry, and galled by a heavy fire from our infantry and artillery, which quickly found the range.

We heard later that the Germans were in very great force, and had attacked in the hope of driving us back, and so uncovering the French left, but they got more than they bargained for. Their losses were terrible in what little of the fight we saw, and when our men captured the guns there was hardly a German left alive or unwounded. Altogether the fight lasted about seven hours, and when it was over our cavalry scouts reported that the enemy were in retreat.

A Coldstream Guardsman, writing of the fighting near the forest of Compiègne, compares the sight of the Germans issuing from the trees to a cup final crowd at the Crystal Palace:

You couldn't miss them. Our bullets ploughed into them, but still they came for us. I was well entrenched, and my rifle got so hot I could hardly hold it. I was wondering if I should have enough bullets when a pal shouted, 'Up, Guards, and at 'em!' The next second he was rolled over with a nasty knock on the shoulder. He jumped up and hissed, 'Let me get at them!' His language was a bit stronger than that.

"When we really did get the order to get at them we made no mistake, I can tell you. They cringed at the bayonet, but those on our left wing tried to get round us, and after racing as hard as we could for quite three hundred yards we cut up nearly every man who did not run away.

Referring to the cavalry, he writes:—

You have read of the charge of the Light Brigade. It was nothing to our chaps. I saw two of our fellows who were unhorsed stand back to back and slash away with their swords, bringing down nine or ten of the panic-stricken devils. Then they got hold of the stirrup-straps of a horse without a rider, and got out of the *mêlée*. This kind of thing was going on all day.

In the afternoon I thought we should all get bowled over, as they came for us again in their big numbers. Where they came from, goodness knows; but as we could not stop them with bullets they had another taste of the bayonet. My captain, a fine fellow, was near to me, and as he fetched them down he shouted, 'Give them socks, my lads!' How many were killed and wounded I don't know; but the field was covered with them.

Private Walter Morton, of the 1st Battalion Black Watch, gave a description of a magnificent charge by his regiment at St. Quentin to the *Scotsman*, Private Morton, who is only 19 years of age, belongs to Camelon, Falkirk:—

We went straight from Boulogne to Mons, being one of the first British regiments to reach that place. Neither army seemed to have a very good position there, but the numbers of the Germans were far too great to give us any chance of success. We were hard at it all day on the Monday, and on Tuesday, as the French reinforcements which we had been expecting did not arrive, the order was given to retire.

In our retreat we marched close upon eighty miles. We passed through Cambrai, and a halt was called at St. Quentin. The Germans, in their mad rush to get to Paris, had seldom been far behind us, and when we came to St. Quentin the word went through the ranks that we were going into action. The men were quite jubilant at the prospect. They had not been at all pleased at their continued retirement before the enemy, and they at once started to get things ready. The engagement opened briskly, both our artillery and the Germans going at it for all they were worth. We were in good skirmishing order, and under the cover of our guns we were all the time getting nearer and nearer the enemy. When we had come to within 100 yards of the German lines the commands were issued for a charge, and the Black Watch made the charge along with the Scots Greys. Not far from us the 9th Lancers and the Cameronians joined in the attack.

It was the finest thing I ever saw. The Scots Greys galloped forward with us hanging on to their stirrups, and it was a sight never to be forgotten. We were simply being dragged by the horses as they flew forward through a perfect cloud of bullets from the enemy's maxims. All other sounds were drowned by the thunder of the horses' hoofs as they careered wildly on, some of them nearly driven mad by the bullets which struck them. It was no time for much thinking. Saddles were being emptied quickly as we closed on the German lines, and tore past their maxims, which were in the front ranks.

We were on the German gunners before they knew where they were, and many of them went down in their gore, scarcely realising that we were amongst them. Then the fray commenced in deadly earnest. The Black Watch and the Scots Greys went into it like men possessed. They fought like demons. It was our bayonets against the Germans' swords. You could see nothing but the glint of steel, and soon even that was wanting as our boys got well into the midst of the enemy. The German swords were no use against us, and just clashed against the bayonets as the now bloodstained steel was sent well home time and again. They went down in hundreds, and still the deadly work of the bayonet continued.

The enemy began to waver as the carnage amongst them increased, and they soon broke and fled before the bayonets like rabbits before the shot of a gun. Still the slaughter went on, with here and there a fierce hand-to-hand exchange, where Germans with their retreat cut off fought to the last. We knew what our men had come through, and we did not forget them.

There were about 1,900 of us in that charge against 20,000 Germans, and the charge itself lasted about four hours. We took close upon 4,000 prisoners, and captured a lot of their guns. In the course of the fighting I got a cut from a German sword—they are very much like saws—and fell into a pool of water, where I lay unconscious for twenty-three hours. I was picked up by one of the 9th Lancers.

The *Liberté* gives the following details of the German occupation of Péronne:—

The Germans arrived outside Péronne on August 28, at five in the afternoon. French Dragoons and Alpine regiments fought with the greatest courage to oppose their advance, and enabled the French troops to retire in good order. The Germans had guns in position in the woods at Racogne, overlooking Péronne, and from the east, on the left bank of the Somme, they shelled the town, which greatly suffered.

The enemy entered Péronne at 5.30. The soldiers behaved disgracefully, shouting madly and firing shots at windows, in order to terrorise the inhabitants. At the Town Hall they summoned the authorities, and as none came forward the Germans burned the sub-prefecture building and surrounding houses, after having thrown petrol over them with pumps and then using grenades.

The whole of the main square would have been completely destroyed, had it not been for the courageous intervention of a priest. Canon Caron, who, after an interview with the German officers, succeeded in obtaining a promise that the passage of the enemy through Péronne should not be marked by the complete destruction of this ancient town.

Three inhabitants were selected to take over the administration of the town, and the Germans asked for four hostages, who, however, were released after three days. During the occupation, which lasted from August 27 till September 14, the Germans behaved in the most arbitrary manner. They were constantly requisitioning provisions, and searched and looted all houses and shops, and they sent back to Germany whole trains filled with furniture stolen from deserted houses.

On September 5 the head doctor of the German ambulance gave orders to send to Amiens all the French wounded. The Amiens Red Cross sent twenty automobiles, with doctors and nurses, and the latter were on the point of restarting for Amiens when Colonel von Kosser, the governor of the town, ordered them to be detained in Péronne, where they remained for two days in barracks, and were then released. The Red Cross people had to walk to Amiens, as the Germans kept the motor-cars. On September 14 Colonel von Kosser hurriedly left the town, and the next morning a division of French cavalry reoccupied the place.

The Germans left so precipitately that they had to abandon the wounded and the ambulances. The staff of the latter consisted of seventy women, twenty-five doctors, 150 assistants, a Protestant chaplain, a Franciscan chaplain, and a few sisters. The latter were armed with heavy revolvers, which a German doctor said was to ensure the protection of their persons.

In spite of such a gross violation of the Geneva Convention, the personnel of the ambulances were treated with the greatest respect. The women were disarmed, and the ambulance, which was splendidly organised, was sent by special train to Switzerland.

The *Daily Telegraph* correspondent described how the English, in their retirement, came like an avalanche on Chantilly, followed closely by the Germans, after evacuating Compiègne. His informant was an English trainer who escaped with his wife under the fire of the German guns, leaving all his fine racehorses, goods, and chattels behind.

It was on Sunday last, August 30, he said, that the firing which had been coming nearer and nearer La Croix Saint-Ouen made him hurry into Compiègne to learn what was going on. He was surprised to find Compiègne become the headquarters of the retiring British Army. The sight was one of the most extraordinary he had ever seen.

At a place I am not at liberty to mention he was suddenly met by what he calls an invasion of all that might be called English. First the motor vans appeared. All London, Manchester, and Liverpool seemed to be on the roads. English brewery vans and London motor-'buses with advertisements still on some of them led the way. Along came the vans of well-known firms like an avalanche. They raced down the roads, tooted without stopping, and made a deafening noise that echoed all over the forest.

Provisions, guns, and ammunition were conveyed as fast as they could to the place assigned them in the rear. The drivers seemed to know the roads as if they had been over them every day for years.

When they reached the place assigned to them they got out, prepared to lay down and sleep on the roadside, and told each other funny stories to while away the time. One of the last who had come into Compiègne had missed his way. Suddenly he came upon a few Germans whom he mistook at first for English soldiers. He looked more closely, and when only within a few hundred yards he recognised his mistake. He instantly wheeled his van round, and before they were able to open fire he was racing down the road as if devils were behind him. ' I got my van away all right and I laughed at their popping at me,' he said.

After the vans came the soldiers, headed by the 5th Dragoons. They had blown up everything behind them, railway lines and bridges, and it would be some time before the Germans would come up. The soldiers as they reached Compiègne were in the best of spirits. They had been fighting all the time, killing scores of the enemy as they retired through the woods, and losing hardly a man themselves. The French people in all the villages and at Compiègne received them with a hearty welcome.

When they came to an inn or a '*marchand de vin*,' they were offered any drink in the shop for nothing, or what they liked to give. As a rule the barmen offered them the best wine. The soldiers would smell it, nod their heads, as much as to convey 'this is good,' and down it would go. 'Fine drink that,' they would say to each other, and march off again.

At Compiègne all the townsfolk came out, and exclaimed: 'What fine men, these English!' The fact is the people here, as well as at Chantilly, were accustomed to see, as a rule, only English jockeys and stable lads, of less than average size. They had thereby come to imagine that Englishmen mostly were smaller than the French. When they saw the dragoons and lancers and the Scottish troops and Highlanders, they wondered, and were beside themselves with admiration.

In the shops the English soldiers made it a point to pay for everything they got. Funny scenes were often witnessed. They would select anything they fancied, hold it up in their hands, and ask mutely by a sign 'How much?' Sometimes misunderstandings occurred. Tommy Atkins had not yet had time to master the simplicity of French currency. Two of them were buying bread. One paid for his, and the other laid down the same amount, thinking it was all right. The loaf was much bigger, and the baker tried to explain to him that it was two pounds. 'What,' exclaimed the indignant trooper, 'two pounds for a loaf of bread. You are trying it on,' and out he walked indignantly, clinging to his loaf nevertheless. Finally, it was explained to him what the baker meant, namely, that it weighed two pounds. The soldier at once asked a pal to return and apologise, and, as he said, 'pay up and tell the tale.'

The Germans did not give them time to stay long at Compiègne. Firing was resumed during the night, and on Monday afternoon, August 31, the enemy was already swarming round La Croix-Saint-Ouen and La Morlay. In the withdrawal the English were accompanied by French *chasseurs* Alpins, and the country in the valley of the Oise, with its steep slopes, afforded them good opportunities of inflicting losses on the enemy.

The alarm of the advancing Germans had reached Chantilly.

People went from house to house to spread the news. Most of the trainers had already left and their horses had also been got away. Still about forty or fifty animals remained in the stables. On Tuesday, September 1, the guns were heard at Chantilly. Fighting was then going on around Creil, which the Germans had reached. The English soldiers fell back methodically, eating and sleeping on the roadside, and turning back to have a shot at the enemy. He lent himself easily to this game by coming on in dense columns.

The soldiers have wonderful tales about the execution done by the Maxim guns. 'We take up a position on the roadside and wait for them to come,' said one of them. 'When they are 200 or 300 yards away we are eager to fire. "Wait a bit," says the captain, "till I make sure they are not English." He looks through his field-glasses, and then says, " Let 'em have it, boys!" Off it goes, and you see fifty or sixty of them fellows drop. They don't care; others come on, and then we move our gun.'

This is the kind of fighting that was going on for three days in the forests of Compiègne and Chantilly. They cover about 50,000 acres of ground, and lend themselves wonderfully to small skirmishes. The woods are cut in every direction by lanes and training paths, which were used by the Germans. They even moved their artillery over them; in fact, they swarmed everywhere. On Tuesday evening Chantilly was empty." The frightful odds which the Germans, knowing the quality of our troops, threw against our lines, caused a withdrawal to a new position.

A Press Bureau statement says:

> After this engagement our troops were no longer molested. Wednesday, September 2, was the first quiet day they had had since the fighting had begun at Mons on August 23.

During the whole of this period marching and fighting had been continuous, and in the whole period the British casualties had amounted, according to the latest estimates, to about 15,000 officers and men.

The fighting having been in open order upon a wide front, with repeated retirements, led to a large number of officers and men, and even small parties, missing their way and getting separated, and it was known that a very considerable number of those included in the total would rejoin the colours safely.

These losses, though heavy in so small a force, in no wise affected the spirit of the troops.

They did not amount to a third of the losses inflicted by the British force upon the enemy, and the sacrifice required of the Army had not been out of proportion to its military achievements.

In all, drafts amounting to 19,000 men reached our Army, or were approaching them on the line of communication, and advantage was taken of the five quiet days that had passed since the action of September 1 to fill up the gaps and refit and consolidate the units.

The German Army on September 2 was described as having:

> .... gradually narrowed its principal attacking point, until it had become an arrow-head or a V-shaped mass pointing directly for Paris, and the southern-most end of the enemy was just before Creil, less than an hour's run from the capital by train. Before it was a river, bridges awaiting to be blown up, an army as ready as ever to resist it, and the fortifications of Paris. Away on the sloping flanks were armies of the Allies, numerically inferior but as full of fight as their opponents.

But the Germans had advanced further south than Creil for on the night of September 1 their patrols were in action at Senlis with an infantry brigade of the Allies.

It is curious to note that this quiet day was the forty-fourth anniversary of the battle of Sedan, when it was expected that the Germans would have made a desperate effort—sparing no sacrifices to repeat the triumph of 1870. But the conditions that prevailed on September 2, 1914, were not quite the same. Sedan-day was, however, celebrated in Berlin, where demonstrations were said to have taken place of a character highly satisfactory to the public.

The fighting at this place was severe, as is testified by the Rev. F. Anstruther Cardew, Chaplain of St. George's, Paris, who recently paid a visit to the battlefields of the Aisne.

> Our route lay through Senlis, a beautiful old-world town with its venerable cathedral and monastery. I knew that the Germans had occupied this place and done much damage, but I was not prepared for what I saw. The quarter of the town through which we drove was utterly wrecked, every single house without exception was smashed to pieces by shells and gutted by fire; nothing was left to tell the passage of the German army but blackened and desolate rubble and masonry.

Other quarters of the town, however, do not appear to have suffered so heavily.

Mr. W. Maxwell, writing from Beauvais, on Wednesday, September 2, supplied the following able article on the retirement of the British Expeditionary Forces:—

I have just returned from the direction of Rheims, and have met some of the men who have been fighting in the north. The last time I saw them was on Saturday, August 22, when they were marching on Mons. Their lines stretched east toward Charleroi and west toward Tournai through Valenciennes, and army headquarters were at Le Cateau, about sixty miles to the south.

Since then they have fought a great battle and fallen back fighting over a distance of nearly 100 miles. Yet it is just the same confident and cheerful army it was ten days ago.

The retirement must have been a fearful ordeal. Everybody is aware of the tremendous efforts the enemy have been making to strike at the capital of France. They have been content with demonstrations on the east and with masking the fortress positions along that border; they have descended in hordes from the north; they have poured out their blood like water from the Meuse to the Somme; but they have reserved their greatest efforts and sacrifices for the northwest.

It is this turning movement on the left flank of the British that has forced the allied armies to retire. Never was attack made with more reckless courage nor pressed with such relentless ferocity. And never was defence conducted with greater heroism. Every mile has been contested with stubborn gallantry, British and French retiring with their faces to the foe.

Their numbers were overwhelming. They gave us no rest. Night and day they hammered away, coming on like great waves. The gaps we made were filled instantly. Their artillery, which is well handled, played upon us incessantly. Their cavalry swept down upon us with amazing recklessness. If we have heavy losses the enemy have even greater.

Officers tell me that our men fought with cool gallantry. They never wavered an instant. But the pressure was irresistible. Column after column, squadron after squadron, mass after mass, the enemy came on like a battering ram crushing everything in its way. Shattered to fragments by shot and shell, the hordes of the enemy seemed instantly to renew themselves; they swarmed on all sides. Nothing but the sheer pluck, the steadfast courage and the unflinching determination of our soldiers saved the army from annihilation.

The losses inflicted on the enemy must have been enormous. They attacked in solid formation, and whole brigades of infantry were decimated by the fire of our rifles and guns. No army of civilised men can endure such devastation as was wrought among the Germans in this long battle over scores of miles.

The retirement was effected with admirable coolness and skill. The positions of the covering troops were well chosen, and our guns shelled the advancing columns until the dead lay in heaps along the roads and in the fields.

A wounded soldier, who insisted on remaining in the ranks said:

The enemy hung on to us like grim death. They wanted us to retire in a direction they had determined upon. But we were not taking our marching orders from them. We went our own way, and at our own pace. We were retiring—not retreating.

Remembering the tremendous difficulties of carrying out a retirement under such conditions, it is amazing how well the men held together. Their losses were great, but not nearly so great as the circumstances seemed to exact. Many of the missing men found their way back to their regiments, from which they were separated in the desperate rush of the fighting.

The attack on the French Army on our right seems to have been heaviest in the neighbourhood of St. Quentin. But the French met it with courage and coolness, sweeping the ranks with their artillery, and advancing with the bayonet under covering fire. For a time they were able to resume the offensive, and drove thousands of the enemy across the river.

But here, as on the left wing, the story was the same. The numbers of the enemy seemed inexhaustible. No sooner was one column wiped out than another was there to take its place. There was nothing for it but to retire fighting.

In continuation of the deeply interesting despatch of Sir John French of September 17, the first portion of which is quoted at the beginning of this chapter, he says:—

GERMAN UHLAN CHARGE

On the 1st September, when retiring from the thickly-wooded country to the south of Compiègne, the 1st Cavalry Brigade was overtaken by some German cavalry. They momentarily lost a Horse Artillery battery, and several officers and men were killed and wounded. With the help, however, of some detachments from the 3rd Corps operating on their left, they not only recovered their own guns but succeeded in capturing 12 of the enemy's.

Similarly, to the eastward, the 1st Corps, retiring south, also got into some very difficult forest country, and a somewhat severe rearguard action ensued at Villers-Cotterets, in which the 4th Guards Brigade suffered considerably.

On September 3rd the British Forces were in position south of the Marne between Lagny and Signy-Signets. Up to this time I had been requested by General Joffre to defend the passages of the river as long as possible, and to blow up the bridges in my front. After I had made the necessary dispositions, and the destruction of the bridges had been effected, I was asked by the French commander-in-chief to continue my retirement to a point some 12 miles in rear of the position I then occupied, with a view to taking up a second position behind the Seine. This retirement was duly carried out. In the meantime the enemy had thrown bridges and crossed the Marne in considerable force, and was threatening the Allies all along the line of the British Forces and the 5th and 9th French Armies. Consequently several small outpost actions took place.

On Saturday, September 5, I met the French commander-in-chief at his request, and he informed me of his intention to take the offensive forthwith, as he considered conditions were very favourable to success.

General Joffre announced to me his intention of wheeling up the left flank of the 6th Army, pivoting on the Marne and directing it to move on the Ourcq; cross and attack the flank of the 1st German Army, which was then moving in a south-easterly direction east of that river.

He requested me to effect a change of front to my right—my left resting on the Marne and my right on the 5th Army—to fill the gap between that army and the 6th. I was then to advance against the enemy in my front and join in the general offensive movement.

These combined movements practically commenced on Sunday, September 6th, at sunrise; and on that day it may be said that a great battle opened on a front extending from Ermenonville, which was just in front of the left flank of the 6th French Army, through Lizy on the Marne, Mauperthuis, which was about the British centre, Courtaçon, which was the left of the 5th French Army, to Esternay and Charleville, the left of the 9th Army under General Foch, and so along the front of the 9th, 4th, and 3rd French Armies to a point north of the fortress of Verdun.

This battle, in so far as the 6th French Army, the British Army, the 5th French Army, and the 9th French Army were concerned, may be said to have concluded on the evening of September 10, by which time the Germans had been driven back to the line Soissons-Reims, with a loss of thousands of prisoners, many guns, and enormous masses of transport.

About the 3rd September the enemy appears to have changed his plans and to have determined to stop his advance south direct upon Paris, for on the 4th September air reconnaissances showed that his main columns were moving in a south-easterly direction generally east of a line drawn through Nanteuil and Lizy on the Ourcq.

On the 5th September several of these columns were observed to have crossed the Marne, whilst German troops, which were observed moving south-east up the left flank of the Ourcq on the 4th, were now reported to be halted and facing that river. Heads of the enemy's columns were seen crossing at Changis, La Ferté, Nogent, Château Thierry, and Mezy.

Considerable German columns of all arms were seen to be converging on Montmirail, whilst before sunset large bivouacs of the enemy were located in the neighbourhood of Coulommiers, south of Rebais, La Ferté-Gaucher, and Dagny.

I should conceive it to have been about noon on the 6th September, after the British Forces had changed their front to the right and occupied the line Jouy—Le Chatel—Faremoutiers—Villeneuve Le Comte, and the advance of the 6th French Army north of the Marne towards the Ourcq became apparent, that the enemy realised the powerful threat that was being made against the flank of his columns moving south-east, and began the great retreat which opened the battle above referred to.

On the evening of the 6th September, therefore, the fronts and positions of the opposing armies were roughly as follows:—

ALLIES.

6th French Army,—Right on the Marne at Meux, left towards Betz.

British Forces,—On the line Dagny—Coulommiers—Maison.

5th French Army,—At Courtagon, right on Esternay.

Conneau's Cavalry Corps,—Between the right of the British and the left of the French 5th Army.

GERMANS.

4th Reserve and 2nd Corps,—East of the Ourcq and facing that river.

9th Cavalry Division,—West of Crecy.

2nd Cavalry Division,—North of Coulommiers.

4th Corps,—Rebais.

3rd and 7th Corps,—South-west of Montmirail.

All these troops constituted the 1st German Army, which was directed against the French 6th Army on the Ourcq, and the British Forces, and the left of the 5th French Army south of the Marne.

The 2nd German Army (IX., X., X.R., and Guard) was moving against the centre and right of the 5th French Army and the 9th French Army.

On the 7th September both the 5th and 6th French Armies were heavily engaged on our flank. The 2nd and 4th Reserve German Corps on the Ourcq vigorously opposed the advance of the French towards that river, but did not prevent the 6th Army from gaining some headway, the Germans themselves suffering serious losses. The French 5th Army threw the enemy back to the line of the Petit Morin River after inflicting severe losses upon them, especially about Montçeaux, which was carried at the point of the bayonet.

The enemy retreated before our advance, covered by his 2nd and 9th and Guard Cavalry Divisions, which suffered severely.

Our cavalry acted with great vigour, especially General de Lisle's Brigade with the 9th Lancers and 18th Hussars.

On the 8th September the enemy continued his retreat northward, and our army was successfully engaged during the day with strong rearguards of all arms on the Petit Morin River, thereby materially assisting the progress of the French Armies on our right and left, against whom the enemy was making his greatest efforts. On both sides the enemy was thrown back with very heavy loss. The 1st Army Corps encountered stubborn resistance at La Trétoire (north of Rebais). The enemy occupied a strong position with infantry and guns on the northern bank of the Petit Morin River; they were dislodged with considerable loss. Several machine guns and many prisoners were captured, and upwards of two hundred German dead were left on the ground.

The forcing of the Petit Morin at this point was much assisted by the cavalry and the 1st Division, which crossed higher up the stream.

Later in the day a counter-attack by the enemy was well repulsed by the 1st Army Corps, a great many prisoners and some guns again falling into our hands.

On this day (8th September) the 2nd Army Corps encountered considerable opposition, but drove back the enemy at all points with great loss, making considerable captures.

The 3rd Army Corps also drove back considerable bodies of the enemy's infantry and made some captures.

On the 9th September the 1st and 2nd Army Corps forced the passage of the Marne and advanced some miles to the north of it. The 3rd Corps encountered considerable opposition, as the bridge at La Ferté was destroyed and the enemy held the town on the opposite bank in some strength, and thence persistently obstructed the construction of a bridge; so the passage was not effected until after nightfall.

During the day's pursuit the enemy suffered heavy loss in killed and wounded, some hundreds of prisoners fell into our hands and a battery of eight machine guns was captured by the 2nd Division.

On this day the 6th French Army was heavily engaged west of the River Ourcq. The enemy had largely increased his force opposing them; and very heavy fighting ensued, in which the French were successful throughout.

The left of the 5th French Army reached the neighbourhood of Château Thierry after the most severe fighting, having driven the enemy completely north of the river with great loss.

The fighting of this army in the neighbourhood of Montmirail was very severe.

The advance was resumed at daybreak on the 10th up to the line of the Ourcq, opposed by strong rearguards of all arms. The 1st and 2nd Corps, assisted by the cavalry division on the right, the 3rd and 5th Cavalry Brigades on the left, drove the enemy northwards. Thirteen guns, seven machine guns, about 2,000 prisoners, and quantities of transport fell into our hands. The enemy left many dead on the field. On this day the French 5th and 6th Armies had little opposition.

As the 1st and 2nd German Armies were now in full retreat, this evening marks the end of the battle which practically commenced on the morning of the 6th instant; and it is at this point in the operations that I am concluding the present despatch.

Although I deeply regret to have had to report heavy losses in killed and wounded throughout these operations, I do not think they have been excessive in view of the magnitude of the great fight, the outlines of which I have only been able very briefly to describe, and the demoralisation and loss in killed and wounded which are known to have been caused to the enemy by the vigour and severity of the pursuit.

In concluding this despatch I must call your Lordship's special attention to the fact that from Sunday, August 23rd, up to the present date (September 17th), from Mons back almost to the Seine, and from the Seine to the Aisne, the army under my command has been ceaselessly engaged without one single day's halt or rest of any kind.

CHAPTER 7

The German Advance on Paris

On September 2 the Germans were in the neighbourhood of Senlis, which is situated only 30 miles from Paris. The advance of the enemy had been steady and it seemed certain that in the course of a day, or at most two, the advance guard would have reached the line of the outer fortifications of the capital. The lines of the Allies were still unbroken, and they were falling back methodically and in good order. The enemy had failed in cutting off and destroying them, but that they intended to siege Paris seemed inevitable. And in this event the city would be placed entirely under military rule. It was essential, therefore, that the government should avoid being bottled up in the city. As happened in 1870, for these reasons the French Government decided to quit Paris for the time being and proceeded to Bordeaux, and before doing so, on September 2, the following proclamation was addressed to the country by the president and ministers:—

> For several weeks sanguinary combats have taken place between our heroic troops and the enemy's army. The bravery of our soldiers has gained for them at several points marked successes, but to the north the pressure of the German forces has compelled us to retire.
>
> This situation imposes upon the President of the Republic and the government the painful decision that in order to watch over the national safety the duty of the authorities is to leave Paris.
>
> Under the command of an eminent leader, a French army full of courage will defend the capital and the patriotic population against the invader; but the war must be continued at the same time on the rest of the territory without peace or truce, with-

out stay or weakness.

The sacred struggle for the honour of the nation and reparation for violated right will continue.

None of our armies has been broken. If some have sustained too perceptible losses, the gaps will be immediately filled from the depots, and the call for recruits assures us for the morrow new resources in men and energy to endure and fight.

That must be the watchword of the allied British, Russian, Belgian, and French armies—to endure and to fight whilst on the sea the British aid us to cut the communications of our enemies with the world; to endure and to fight whilst the Russians continue to advance to deal a decisive blow at the heart of the German Empire.

To the Government of the Republic belongs the duty of directing this stubborn resistance everywhere for French independence.

To give this formidable struggle all its ardour and all its efficacy it is indispensable that the government should remain free to act on the demand of the military authorities.

The government is removing its residence to a point where it can remain in constant relations with the whole of the country.

The National Government does not leave Paris without having assured the defence of the city and the entrenched camp by all the means in its power. The government knows there is no need to advise the Parisian population to calmness, resolution, and coolness.

Frenchmen, be worthy in these tragic circumstances. We shall obtain a final victory. We shall obtain it by untiring will, by endurance and tenacity.

A nation which does not desire to perish, and which wishes to live, recoils neither before suffering nor sacrifices, is sure of conquering.

Although a large number of the inhabitants had left the capital, those who remained maintained a calm demeanour. There was no panic, only strenuous preparations for an energetic defence. Some of the public buildings, including the Louvre, had been protected above against damage from shells or bombs dropped from aircraft, and the most valued treasures of that museum had been withdrawn to a place of safety.

A correspondent of the Central News wrote from Paris:—

Few of the thousands of artists and art-lovers who have been wont to visit the Louvre daily for instruction or pleasure would recognise their haunt now. For the last four weeks the staff has been working hard to carry out the measures ordered for the protection of the chief works of art from what a French paper says is the only danger that menaces them—aerial bombs.

In 1870 the "Venus" of Milo was walled up in a subterranean niche. The advance of civilisation has evolved a more prosaic and more effective protection, and she is now enclosed in a steel room. The "Winged Victory" is sheltered behind heavy iron plates, and the "Gioconda" smiles in obscurity as inscrutably as ever. The Grecian Hall, which contains the masterpieces of Phidias, is protected by sacks filled with earth against any aerial attack. The upper stories of the Louvre, with their glass roofs, have been turned into hospitals, and the flag of the Red Cross protects the works which remain there.

Many paintings and statues have been transferred from the Luxembourg to the old Seminaire, which will henceforth contain the collection, and in all the other galleries, both private and public, the treasures of art are being hidden underground or placed behind heavy screens.

Even with such a danger as a siege imminent, it was recognised that the enemy's task was very great. His object was obviously to push on to Paris as rapidly as possible in order to disturb the preparations for the defence of the city. M. Millerand, however, from the first day of taking office, ordered Paris to be got ready for immediate defence; while General Gallieni, an excellent commander and administrator, lost no time, and the work of preparing the defences proceeded without intermission, day and night. As the Paris correspondent of the *Daily Telegraph* said:—

Only an army of two million men could invest the entrenched camp of Paris with its outlying forts. The very worst eventuality to be considered is a successful raid of the vanguard of what may be left of the German advancing column into Paris. The German advance has undoubtedly been very strong, and has not been withstood with success anywhere up till now. The rush may at this moment have been stopped. Should it not be, and should the desperate onrush of a certain number of German army corps break through the French Army, the enemy would come up against the forts surrounding Paris.

Should the German advance column reach these forts, it will arrive there already to some extent spent, and certainly with its line of communication cut off. If there is a battle outside the forts of Paris it will be a desperate encounter, and it is not likely that the German force engaged will live to tell the tale.

In describing the fortifications of Paris, he says:—

The defensive works forming the almost impregnable perimeter of forts and earthworks around Paris would be nearly impossible to invest by an invading army with a field army in opposition, or would require an enormous army for the purpose. There are three lines of defences round Paris—the first is the belt of old fortification encircling the city, and built under the premiership of M. Thiers in the reign of Louis Philippe, and these old walls and earthworks were of little use in 1870. Since 1878 a second ring of fortified positions was built, though it does not form a continuous circumference of defensive positions, but several separate fortresses.

The threatened approach to Paris lies to the north, therefore these may be described first. A number of very strong positions lie between the Oise and the Seine—the middle of these powerful lines resting mostly on hilly eminences in the Forest of Montmorency. The backbone, so to speak, of these defensive works is composed of a number of forts. Beginning with the defences of the Seine, we have the Fort of Cormeilles, with the Redoubt of Francaville in front, as well as that of Les Cotillons supported throughout by a number of batteries. The strong fortified position of Cormeilles stands at nearly 500 feet above the Seine. The slopes are steep, and for defence these groups are of great power.

The Valley of Ermont lies between the great works of Cormeilles and the Forest of Montmorency, but these forts and those of Montlignon and Montmorency, placed on the southwest fringe of the forest, sweep the valley. At the north-east of the forest is the Fort of Domont, and further on a pile covered with trees, another strong defensive group exists, including the Fort of Ecouen and several connected batteries.

THE FORTS AROUND PARIS

Southwards are the Forts of Stains and the battery of Pincon Hill. This remarkably powerful fortress, with its dependent defences composed of batteries, permanent trenches, timber-cleared expanses for shooting, and barbed wire fences, render it secure against a surprise attack. To the east of St. Denis there is a low-lying plain showing no favourable point for fortification, but which can be flooded by the Rivers Morée and the Trond. This plain is also exposed to the fire of the Fort of Stains and the battery of the "Butte Pincon," and the defensive works of Vaujours to the south.

The Fort of Vaujours and that of Chelles bar access to Paris in the passage between the "*Canal de l'Durque*" and the Marne. Higher up the Marne than Chelles, and between that river and the Seine, the Forts of Villiers, Champigny, Sucy, and Villeneuve St. Georges have been constructed. These fortified bulwarks of Paris are exceedingly strong. The defensive lines on the Marne from Chelles to Charenton form a rampart against any surprise rush, and as the positions of Montmorency and between Vaujours and Chelles, the fixed defences, have been greatly strengthened by batteries, felled timber and trenches, wire obstacles, and other devices, a most determined resistance could be made in this "sector" of fortified positions. Some improvised field works have been constructed all round Paris, therefore there is no need to describe them in detail.

Between the Seine and Palaiseau there are no permanent fortifications in the wide plain, but no attack could be made in this direction or in the Plain of St. Denis unless the powerful fortifications which can concentrate their fire on these passages had been silenced. The fortifications of an earlier date are completely free from a possible dash and render these zones literal mouse-traps. Like Montmorency, the forts of Palaiseau, Villiers, Haut Buc, Saint Cyr, and the batteries of the Bois de Verrières to the south of Versailles form a real fortress, of which the Fort de Chatillon is the mainstay behind.

Behind Versailles and St. Germain, the Forest of Marly is literally enclosed by batteries outlying the extreme strong works of "*Le Trou de Fer*." Behind this group stands the high and prominent fort of Mont Valérien, which still maintains great military value for defence.

While Paris was waiting for the approach of the enemy, he altered his plans and made an unexpected move. As Sir John French said in his despatch of September 15:—

On Friday, September 4, it became apparent that there was an alteration in the direction of advance of almost the whole of the First Germany Army. That army, since the battle near Mons, on August 23, had been playing its part in the colossal strategic endeavour to create a Sedan for the Allies by outflanking and enveloping the left of their whole line, so as to encircle and drive both British and French to the south. There was now a change in its objective; and it was observed that the German forces opposite the British were beginning to move in a south-easterly direction, instead of continuing south-west on the capital.

Leaving a strong rearguard along the line of the River Ourcq (which flows south, and joins the Marne at Lizy-sur-Ourcq) to keep off the French 6th Army, which by then had been formed, and was to the north-west of Paris, they were evidently executing what amounted to a flank march diagonally across our front. Prepared to ignore the British, as being driven out of the fight, they were initiating an effort to attack the left flank of the French main army, which stretched in a long curved line from our right towards the east, and so to carry out against it alone the envelopment which had so far failed against the combined forces of the Allies.

On Saturday, the 5th, this movement on the part of the Germans was continued, and large advanced parties crossed the Marne, southwards at Trilport, Sammeroy, La Ferté-sous-Jouarre, and Château Thierry.

There was considerable fighting with the French 5th Army on the French left, which fell back from its position south of the Marne towards the Seine. On Sunday, the 6th, large hostile forces crossed the Marne and pushed on through Coulommiers past the British right. Farther east they were attacked at night by the French 5th Army, which captured three villages at the point of the bayonet.

On Monday, the 7th, there was a general advance on the part of the Allies in this quarter of the field. Our forces, which had by now been reinforced, pushed on in a north-easterly direction, in co-operation with an advance of the French 5th Army to the north and of the French 6th Army eastwards, against the German rearguard along the Ourcq.

Possibly weakened by the detachment of troops to the eastern theatre of operations, and realising that the action of the French 6th Army against the line of the Ourcq and the advance of the British placed their own flanking movement in considerable danger of being taken in rear and on its right flank, the Germans on this day commenced to retire towards the north-east. This was the first time that these troops had turned back since their attack at Mons a fortnight before, and from reports received, the order to retreat when so close to Paris was a bitter disappointment. From letters found on the dead there is no doubt that there was a general impression amongst the enemy's troops that they were about to enter Paris.

On Tuesday, the 8th, the German movement north-eastwards was continued, their rearguards on the south of the Marne being pressed back to that river by our troops and by the French on our right, the latter capturing three villages after a hand-to-hand fight and the infliction of severe losses on the enemy.

The fighting along the Ourcq continued on this day and was of the most sanguinary character, for the Germans had massed a great force of artillery along this line. Very few of their infantry were seen by the French. The French 5th Army also made a fierce attack on the Germans in Montmirail, regaining that place.

On Wednesday, the 9th, the battle between the French 6th Army and what was now the German flank guard along the Ourcq continued. The British corps, overcoming some resistance on the River Petit Morin, crossed the Marne in pursuit of the Germans, who were now hastily retreating northwards. One of our corps was delayed by an obstinate defence made by a strong rearguard with machine guns at La Ferté-sous-Jouarre, where the bridge had been destroyed.

On Thursday, the 10th, the French 6th Army continued its pressure on the west, while the 5th Army, by forced marches, reached the line Château Thierry—Dormans on the Marne. Our troops also continued the pursuit on the north of the latter river, and after a considerable amount of fighting captured some 1,500 prisoners, four guns, six machine guns, and fifty transport wagons.

Many of the enemy were killed and wounded, and the numerous thick woods which dot the country north of the Marne were filled with German stragglers. Most of them appeared to have been without food for at least two days. Indeed, in this area of operations the Germans seemed to be demoralised and inclined to surrender in small parties, and the general situation appeared to be most favourable to the Allies.

Much brutal and senseless damage was done in the villages occupied by the enemy. Property was wantonly destroyed, pictures in the *châteaux* were ripped up, and the houses generally pillaged. It is stated on unimpeachable authority, also, that the inhabitants were much ill-treated.

Interesting incidents occurred during the fighting. On the 10th, part of our 2nd Army Corps advancing north found itself marching parallel with another infantry force at some little distance away. At first it was thought that this was another British unit. After some time, however, it was discovered that it was a body of Germans retreating. Measures were promptly taken to head off the enemy, who were surrounded and trapped in a sunken road, where over 400 men surrendered.

On the 10th a small party of French under a non-commissioned officer was cut off and surrounded. After a desperate resistance it was decided to go on fighting to the end. Finally the N.C.O. and one man only were left, both being wounded. The Germans came up and shouted to them to lay down their arms. The German commander, however, signed to them to keep their arms, and then asked permission to shake hands with the wounded non-commissioned officer, who was carried off on his stretcher with his rifle by his side.

The arrival of the reinforcements and the continued advance delighted the troops, who were full of zeal and anxious to press on.

Quite one of the features of the campaign, on our side, has been the success attained by the Royal Flying Corps. In regard to the collection of information it is impossible either to award too much praise to our aviators for the way they carried out their duties, or to overestimate the value of the intelligence collected, more especially during the recent advance. In due course, certain examples of what has been effected may be specified, and the far-reaching nature of the results fully explained, but that time has not yet arrived.

That the services of our Flying Corps, which has really been on trial, are fully appreciated by our Allies is shown by the following message from the Commander-in-Chief of the French Armies, received on September 9 by Field-Marshal Sir John French:

> Please express most particularly to Marshal French my thanks for services rendered on every day by the English Flying Corps. The precision, exactitude, and regularity of the news brought in by its members are evidence of their perfect organisation, and also of the perfect training of pilots and observers.

To give a rough idea of the amount of work carried out, it is sufficient to mention that during a period of twenty days up to September 10 a daily average of more than nine reconnaissance flights of over 100 miles each had been maintained.

The constant object of our aviators has been to effect the accurate location of the enemy's forces, and incidentally—since the operations cover so large an area—of our own units. Nevertheless, the tactics adopted for dealing with hostile aircraft are to attack them instantly with one or more British machines. This has been so far successful that in five cases German pilots or observers have been shot in the air and their machines brought to ground.

As a consequence, the British Flying Corps has succeeded in establishing an individual ascendancy which is as serviceable to us as it is damaging to the enemy. How far it is due to this cause it is not possible at present to ascertain definitely, but the fact remains that the enemy have recently become much less enterprising in their flights. Something in the direction of the mastery of the air has already been gained.

In pursuance of the principle that the main object of military aviators is the collection of information, bomb dropping has not been indulged in to any great extent. On one occasion a petrol bomb was successfully exploded in a German bivouac at night, while, from a diary found on a dead German cavalry soldier, it has been discovered that a high-explosive bomb thrown at a cavalry column from one of our aeroplanes struck an ammunition wagon. The resulting explosion killed fifteen of the enemy.

Ample evidence has been supplied by the correspondents to the newspapers of the inhuman treatment meted out to civilians by the

Germans. Reference has already been made in the present book to this subject. There is another unworthy characteristic of the Germans by which they exact the utmost penalty from non-combatants. Mr. William Maxwell has illustrated this form of vandalism in the following interesting article contributed to the columns of the *Daily Telegraph*, Apparently the same tale might be told of any village or town in France or Belgium through which the Germans advanced or retreated:—

This is a story of German rage and vengeance, not a story of mere looting. Every army loots—even the British Army will condescend to steal chickens and an occasional sheep. In South Africa Lord Roberts had to threaten severe penalties for raids on private property, and I remember an Australian colonel warning his men in this fashion: "If I catch any one of you stealing and killing a sheep—except in self-defence—" The rest of the threat was never spoken.

At three o'clock on Saturday afternoon, September 5, several thousand of the enemy's cavalry—*Uhlans*, dragoons, and *chasseurs*—with horse artillery and machine guns, rode into the village of Beton-Bazoches, south of the River Marne. At first they behaved well enough toward the inhabitants, most of them paying cash for what they took for themselves, and giving receipts for the stores they requisitioned for the army.

The general and senior members of the staff took possession of the inn, while the junior members occupied the house of a grocer, until a rifle and some ammunition were found on the premises, whereupon they removed to other quarters. The officer who made this discovery acted like a sensible and humane man. He advised the villagers to give up their arms, and said to them:

Remember, I am not *le bon Dieu*, and cannot watch over you always. Those who come after us are hard men."

He was a true prophet. Next day there was a sudden fall in the temperature of the invaders. Something unforeseen and dreadful seemed to have happened, and caused the Germans to abandon those conciliatory methods which they have usually adopted in places they have occupied.

I have always been slow to accept stories of atrocities—having heard them told about every army—and I have never reported one without giving my authority and having a written and signed statement. But what I am now about to describe I have seen with my own eyes.

On Sunday afternoon the German soldiery made the discovery that brigandage is one of the privileges of war. They broke into every house and shop, burst open all doors, ransacked every room from cellar to attic, searched every cupboard and drawer, tore up letters and account books, and carried off every portable article of any value. Beton-Bazoches—when they had gone through it—looked as if an earthquake had struck it and left only the empty shell. The hotel that sheltered and fed the general was not spared. A uniformed ruffian rode up to the door and called loudly for *Madame*, who promptly appeared, and had a revolver clapped to her cheek.

"The key to the wine cellar!" demanded the ruffian. In the twinkling of an eyelid the cellar was emptied, and several hundred bottles of champagne and other wine—if there is any other wine—were at the throats of the German soldiers. The same thing happened elsewhere. Stores and *cafés* were cleared of their stock of wines and liqueurs in bottle and barrel. What the soldiers could not drink or carry away they spilt.

"*Pas une bouteille! Pas une bouteille!*" cried the distracted mayor as he showed me over the devastated cellars of his son-in-law, who had gone to the war. "*Pas une bouteille!*" He emphasised his ejaculation by biting his thumb.

"I gave a dozen bottles of good old wine for the sick and wounded," said the dame of the inn, "but the brigands drank it, laughed in my face, and said, '*Krieg guerre nichts payer.*'" The result of this orgy was that hundreds of German cavalrymen were dead drunk on Sunday, and that fourteen did not recover from their debauch until the French arrived at Beton-Bazoches.

A French dragoon, wandering through the town and hearing snores that sounded like a whole battery of artillery in action, stuck his lance into what looked like a huge parcel wrapped in a blanket. To his amazement the parcel stirred. Another prod of the lance, and there came out of the blanket the head of a bearded *Uhlan*. One more touch of cold steel, and the mouth opened with a roar of laughter.

"*Ja! Ja!*" cried the *Uhlan*, stepping in lively style out of the blanket to avoid another prod of the lance. He was immediately recognised as the ruffian who had taken the key of the inn cellar, and had pleaded war as an excuse for non-payment of his score. He was searched, and on him were found 2,000 *francs*, which had doubtless been stolen.

On Sunday the Germans set fire to the stables and granaries of the modest little *château*, whose owner was absent, and next day they tried to burn some of the houses and shops, but were in too great a hurry to set them alight.

On Monday morning they posted their artillery on a height commanding the road to the west along which the French cavalry was advancing. But the enemy did not wait to be attacked. After firing a few shots they removed the guns to another hill on the east, only to abandon it promptly. Then they rode away, leaving in the village seven killed, twenty-three wounded, and fourteen drunken brigands. As they retired the Germans thrust their lances into the bodies of two wounded French soldiers.

The German wounded were cared for by the villagers. "One of them," said a young Frenchwoman, "was a very pretty boy—a noble, I feel sure. He was shot through the chest, and offered thousands of *marks* for a motorcar to take him to hospital. But we don't take money for services of that kind."

The enemy took with them all the motorcars and bicycles, many of the horses and carts, all the petrol, wine, tobacco, jam and provisions. They killed many sheep and cattle, and kept the village baker busy night and day, with a revolver at his head and a bayonet at his back to prevent him from falling asleep. They cleaned out the shop of the jeweller and watchmaker.

In all the best houses were remnants of interrupted feasts—stumps of cigars that had burned holes in the table-covers, half-empty champagne and liqueur bottles, broken bread, and the remains of chickens and omelettes. Silver was missing, though plated goods were left, for they appear to have a nice taste in such articles also.

The next village, Courtaçon, about eight miles to the south of La Ferté, fared even worse. When I entered between its smoking walls and smouldering hayricks, I was met by a weeping woman.

"They have killed my son—my only son!"

He was a mere boy, and the German soldiers shot him dead as he sat at table by his mother's side.

All the farmsteads, the *gendarmerie*, all the best houses were heaps of burning ruins. The Germans set fire to them before they fled; they shot horses and cattle, they threatened the un-armed villagers with death, and they put the mayor at the head of their retreating column. Courtaçon looked as though it had been disembowelled and thrown to the flames.

The following remarkable disclosure was made by Mr. Granville Fortescue[1] on a victory of the French over the army of the Crown Prince on September 6-7. As it will be seen, this event undoubtedly had the far-reaching result of saving Paris from siege:—

The first German Army to be thoroughly whipped on French soil was that of the crown prince. This saved Paris. And this re-markable piece of news has remained a secret until now. At the time of their victory the French did not know the extent of the damage they had inflicted upon the enemy. In fact, they did not make claim to a decisive victory. In the official communication the most they claimed was a drawn battle. Actually they had smashed the flower of German military power.

Contrary to the general impression the great battles round Paris did not begin with the defeat of General von Kluck. That commander's misfortunes were due directly to the retirement of the German left wing on the night of September 6-7. The mystery which has surrounded the movements of the German armies disappears now that we know that the main body of the crown prince's army retired forty kilometres during that night. Such a retirement amounts to a rout.

In the plan of the German operations, the path that prom-ised the greatest glory was reserved for the crown prince. This was in accordance with the policy of bolstering up the fast fading popularity of the House of Hohenzollern. Throughout Germany he was acclaimed as the hero of Longwy. His futile demonstration against Verdun was magnified into a series of glorious assaults. In official bulletins he was declared to have inflicted a severe defeat on the French. As a matter of fact, the French Army opposed to him has been carrying out a splendid defensive retirement. Opposed by superior numbers they have

---

1. *At the Western Front* by Granville Fortescue: Two Classic Accounts of the First World War by an American Correspondent—*At the Front With Three Armies & France Bears the Burden* is also published by Leonaur.

contested with stubbornness every inch of the ground lost. And in the end they assumed the offensive in a most effective manner.

The Germans advanced on the line Verdun—Ste. Menehould—Chalons-sur-Marne. Their progress was exceedingly rapid. When the *Uhlans* of Kluck's force were in Chantilly the main body of the *Kaiser's* heir's army was yet 200 kilometres away. Then this army was ordered to push on with all speed. The order of march of the German army up the Champs Elysees was being drawn up. And, as the crown prince was to head this historic march, undoubtedly dressed in the uniform of his pet regiment, the Death's Head Hussars, the French troops opposing him must be brushed aside.

The left wing of the Germans gave battle on Sunday, September 6. The fighting began at daybreak, and continued with unprecedented fury until dark. The artillery fire went beyond anything the history of warfare has hitherto recorded. Shells were timed to be falling at the rate of thirty in thirty seconds. I have this from a trustworthy source. In this day's fighting the French guns were served with undeniable superiority. The loss they inflicted upon the Germans can never be approximately estimated. The total loss of the Germans is placed at figures so high I hesitate to record them. One hundred thousand, of whom 20,000 were killed. This estimate is made by a trained observer, who was on the battlefield before the dead had been touched.

It must be remembered that the German army was advancing on a front nearly forty miles in extent, and the country northeast of Sezanne is the most treacherous in all France. Acres upon acres of marsh lands line the valleys. Here it was the enemy suffered most.

But the French also made the most severe sacrifices. A certain corps was practically wiped out of existence. Spurred by the knowledge that they were fighting for the very existence of Paris, each French soldier was as three. Against the desperate resistance they made the Germans could do nothing.

When the night of September 6 closed down neither army could claim much advantage in position gained.

The French had made certain gains, but then they had also fallen back at points. An enormous quantity of ammunition had been used up. The total artillery expenditure is put at 4,000 shells. Hundreds of caissons were empty.

Then, on the night of September 6-7, came the German retreat. The long line was giving way, not only on the right towards Paris, but also on the left, where there seems to have been heavy fighting about Verdun.

It has been suggested that there was a breakdown on the transport service in this direction. If this were the case, after the enormous expenditure of ammunition during the first day of action, the crown prince's army would have been obliged to fall back or be captured.

The circumstances of their precipitate flight incline me to the last explanation. Of course, the fighting on this wing continued for several days, but the Germans were only trying to save what was left of a badly crippled army from complete destruction.

With the crown prince retreating, there was nothing left for von Kluck's and von Bülow's armies but to execute the same manoeuvre. This brought about the Battle of the Aisne and all the subsequent fighting. In the fighting the French have been uniformly successful. It goes without saying that the English troops contributed largely to this success. Their bravery has passed into proverb throughout France.

While I have been studying this extraordinary battlefield I have everywhere met the rumour that in the engagement the *Kaiser's* heir was wounded. Stranger things have happened. Following an army in the field one soon learns to put little credence in the hundred and one stories that spring into life daily. But the story of the wounding of the crown prince has been clothed in so much detail as to make it sound plausible. At any rate, although he himself may be unhurt, his army is hopelessly crippled.

At the moment when the German Army was suffering this defeat, the Allies were taking a step which showed that they were united in the issue as well as the purposes of the war. On September 6 the Foreign Office made public the subjoined important declaration concerning the attitude of the governments of the Triple Entente regarding the terms of peace when the time comes for discussing them:—

DECLARATION.

The undersigned, duly authorised thereto by their respective governments, hereby declare as follows:

The British, French, and Russian Governments mutually engage not to conclude peace separately during the present war. The three governments agree that when terms of peace come to be discussed, no one of the Allies will demand conditions of peace without the previous agreement of each of the other Allies.

In faith whereof the undersigned have signed this declaration and have affixed thereto their seals.

Done at London in triplicate, this 5th day of September, 1914.

  (L.S.)   E. Grey,
    His Britannic Majesty's Secretary
    of State for Foreign Affairs.

  (L.S.)   Paul Cambon,
    Ambassador Extraordinary
    Plenipotentiary of the French Republic.

  (L.S.)   Benckendorff,
    Ambassador Extraordinary and Plenipotentiary
    of his Majesty the Emperor of Russia.

★★★★★★

An attempt has been made in the foregoing pages to tell the story of how the Allied forces retreated towards Paris, after the great battle of August 22-24 at Mons on the Belgian frontier, and continued to withdraw until the battle at Senlis on September 1. This account is chiefly concerned with the actions of the British troops who undoubtedly on the left, by their dogged fighting, had saved the situation during the first critical days. But their natural position having been lost, it was the policy of the Allies to retire, and with entrenched fortifications protecting their left, prepare for a counter attack from the advancing Germans.

For the British the enemy's assault was especially furious, but it failed both in breaking their lines and their spirit. Travel-stained, bearded and unwashed, their courage remained undaunted. The Allies fought as they fell back and fought again, until they met and defeated the army of the crown prince on September 6-7. Here the march of the invader was arrested, and the next episode of the war was the victorious fight against the Germans on the Marne.

The despatches of Sir John French and the official *communiqués* issued by the French War Office supply us with the barest events of the war, but for a picture of the actual fighting and the heroic deeds of our brave men we must turn to the many stories told by the soldiers themselves and other witnesses, some of which we have quoted.

Ever since the South African Campaign the art of war has changed and the combatants in the present campaign are fighting under circumstances that have never before prevailed, in many cases with weapons that have not before been used on the battlefield. Air-craft for reconnaissances, and armed motorcars and motor-bicycles and motor vehicles for transport and other purposes, have gone far towards revolutionising warfare; although introduced in the Balkan war they are being utilised to a much greater extent in the present conflict.

Sufficient has been said incidentally in this book with regard to the German methods of warfare. The justice of our cause has been demonstrated by able statesmen as well as by men of every shade of opinion and creed. Their relentless persecution of the neutral State of Belgium, and their brutal disregard of all recognised canons of humanity, so far from terrorising the Allies, have strengthened their determination to fight to the bitter end Germany the enemy of the world.

LEONAUR

ALSO FROM LEONAUR
AVAILABLE IN SOFTCOVER OR HARDCOVER WITH DUST JACKET

THE 9TH—THE KING'S (LIVERPOOL REGIMENT) IN THE GREAT WAR 1914 - 1918 *by Enos H. G. Roberts*—Mersey to mud—war and Liverpool men.

THE GAMBARDIER *by Mark Severn*—The experiences of a battery of Heavy artillery on the Western Front during the First World War.

FROM MESSINES TO THIRD YPRES *by Thomas Floyd*—A personal account of the First World War on the Western front by a 2/5th Lancashire Fusilier.

THE IRISH GUARDS IN THE GREAT WAR - VOLUME 1 *by Rudyard Kipling*—Edited and Compiled from Their Diaries and Papers—The First Battalion.

THE IRISH GUARDS IN THE GREAT WAR - VOLUME 1 *by Rudyard Kipling*—Edited and Compiled from Their Diaries and Papers—The Second Battalion.

ARMOURED CARS IN EDEN *by K. Roosevelt*—An American President's son serving in Rolls Royce armoured cars with the British in Mesopatamia & with the American Artillery in France during the First World War.

CHASSEUR OF 1914 *by Marcel Dupont*—Experiences of the twilight of the French Light Cavalry by a young officer during the early battles of the great war in Europe.

TROOP HORSE & TRENCH *by R.A. Lloyd*—The experiences of a British Lifeguardsman of the household cavalry fighting on the western front during the First World War 1914-18.

THE EAST AFRICAN MOUNTED RIFLES *by C.J. Wilson*—Experiences of the campaign in the East African bush during the First World War.

THE LONG PATROL *by George Berrie*—A Novel of Light Horsemen from Gallipoli to the Palestine campaign of the First World War.

THE FIGHTING CAMELIERS *by Frank Reid*—The exploits of the Imperial Camel Corps in the desert and Palestine campaigns of the First World War.

STEEL CHARIOTS IN THE DESERT *by S. C. Rolls*—The first world war experiences of a Rolls Royce armoured car driver with the Duke of Westminster in Libya and in Arabia with T.E. Lawrence.

WITH THE IMPERIAL CAMEL CORPS IN THE GREAT WAR *by Geoffrey Inchbald*—The story of a serving officer with the British 2nd battalion against the Senussi and during the Palestine campaign.